The Child,

Its Nature and Relations;

AN ELUCIDATION

OF

Frœbel's Principles of Education.

BY

Matilda H. Kriege.

A FREE RENDERING OF THE GERMAN

OF THE

Baroness Marenholtz-Bülow.

> Come, let us live for our children!—
> FRIEDRICH FRŒBEL.

SECOND EDITION.

NEW YORK:

E. Steiger.

1872.

NOTICE.

The publisher of this book is resolved to expend his best energies in the interest of Education. He has witnessed with lively satisfaction the progress of education in this country; but while appreciating the good that has been done, he agrees in the opinion of many that the system at work is susceptible of improvement. He has embraced the cause of the Kindergarten System, therefore, as best calculated, in his judgment, to inaugurate a thorough educational reform; and he will gladly entertain proposals for the publication of other valuable works on the subject, and cheerfully coöperate with School authorities, associations and individuals, whose aim is the amelioration of the existing modes of education.

Entered according to Act of Congress, in the year 1872, by
E. Steiger,
in the Office of the Librarian of Congress, at Washington.

E. STEIGER, N. Y.,
Electrotyper and Printer.

CONTENTS.

		Page
PREFACE		1
CHAPTER I.	The New Education	5
CHAPTER II.	The Child's Being. Its Relation to Nature, Man, and God	22
CHAPTER III.	The Child's Manifestations	37
CHAPTER IV.	The Child's Education	55
CHAPTER V.	The Child's Education. (Continued)	72
CHAPTER VI.	Frœbel's "Mother Cosseting Songs"	92
CHAPTER VII.	Frœbel's "Mother Cosseting Songs". (Cont'd)	114
CHAPTER VIII.	Fundamental Forms	133
CHAPTER IX.	Reading	143

PREFACE.

This little book appears in answer to many inquiries addressed to me, by letter and personally, concerning FRŒBEL's system. When in Berlin, where my daughter pursued her study of the system under the Baroness MARENHOLTZ, I communicated to one of our American friends, a gentleman of high culture, who was greatly interested in the Kindergarten method, our intention of introducing FRŒBEL's system into America. He heartily approved, but when I suggested that the best way to do this might be to translate or write a book on the subject, he objected: "No," he said, "I would not do that; you know that our people are eminently practical; you must first show them practically what it is, this will excite interest and inquiry, and then people will be ready to read something on the subject. Anything written about it now would fall dead to the ground."

We have followed this friend's advice. We have exemplified FRŒBEL's method in a Kindergarten, have trained teachers to spread the system, and, by the aid of an enthusiastic and devoted friend of the cause, Miss E. P. PEABODY, who years ago became interested in the subject and has in lectures, conversations, and writings given glimpses of FRŒBEL'S ideas, the way has, we think, been well prepared for the advent of this book.

Instead of relying entirely upon my own interpretation of FRŒBEL'S ideas as I have gathered them from his works, I have taken my clew from one of his personal friends and disciples, the noble and highly gifted Baroness MARENHOLTZ-BUELOW,* and have followed her as closely as I deemed her presentation of the subject adapted to the American mind and mode of thought.

FRŒBEL himself was not happy in the expression of his thoughts in writing, and therefore the personal, friendly intercourse which the Baroness had with him, her intuitive understanding of his often hidden meaning, make her works† and teaching of the greatest value.

A French author, M. GUYARD, wrote to the Baroness in 1857 when she was in Paris as follows:

"Accept my warmest and most sincere wishes for the propagation of FRŒBEL'S method. He is perhaps the greatest philosopher of our time, and has found in you what all philosophers need, that is: a woman who understands him, who clothes him with flesh and blood, and makes him alive. I think, I *believe* indeed, that an idea, in order to bear fruit, must have a father

---

* The Baroness is now in Florence, Italy, where she was invited by the Minister of Public Instruction to introduce FRŒBEL'S Kindergarten and Normal Schools for training teachers.

† "*Das Kind und sein Wesen*", of which this book is a free rendering, and "*Die Arbeit und die neue Erziehung*", are the most important.

and a *mother*. Hitherto ideas have had fathers only. As Frœbel's ideas are so likely to find mothers, they will have an immense success. When the ideas of the future shall have become alive in devoted women, the face of the world will be changed."

So I confidently send forth this little volume, and trust that mothers anxious to do the best for their little ones, teachers who are truly and earnestly trying to fulfil their mission, philanthropists whose thoughts are busy in devising means to diminish vice and crime and to lift humanity upon a higher plane, philosophers who are searching for the cause of things, clergymen who do not believe in faith without works,—in short all intelligent persons, may find some helpful suggestions in its pages. It may perhaps be said, there is nothing new in these ideas;—we knew all this long ago. But is not the fact that the truth announced by Frœbel has long been latent in the minds of all, just the evidence we need that it *is* a truth? In one sense there is nothing new under the sun; but a great many apples had fallen before Newton discovered the law of gravitation! A great truth, a great discovery, is not the special property of any one individual, nor is it for any one nation alone; it is for the whole human family and must be of universal application.

In my anxiety to have Frœbel's principles, those on which he based the Kindergarten, rightly understood, and to have many misapprehensions corrected, I may have unduly hastened the publication of this book, and for any defects in form or expression I ask indulgence.

Those familiar with German should not fail to read the original as well as many other very interesting and instructive books on the subject. May God speed the good cause in spite of all human imperfections!

Matilda H. Kriege.

BOSTON, May, 1872.

Preface to the Second Edition.

It is highly gratifying to the publisher that a second edition of this book is so soon and suddenly called for. The absence of the author abroad prevents, however, any alterations being made in the new edition, and to meet the demand it is issued therefore as a literal reprint of the first.

NEW YORK, October 1872.

CHAPTER I.

The New Education.

The process of remodelling society, the reforms that have been going on in the last century, make a reform in education an absolute necessity.

The life of individuals, as of humanity, is not a chance succession of yesterday, to-day and to-morrow; it is no blind game that deals out to generations their lot; it is a connected whole which is ruled by eternal laws of development even as the microscopic world of the drop of water and the countless solar systems of the universe are ruled. Human society is an organism, and its single parts cannot be affected in isolation. What affects one member of this organism, reacts on every other, and therefore on the whole. Great political revolutions, the remodelling of states, social reforms, as well as important discoveries or inventions, the announcement of new truths, deeper insight,— all produce not only changes within circumscribed limits, but necessitate changes, perhaps improvements, progress in *all* realms of life.

How can Education remain unaffected? Has it not to prepare the coming generation for these altered, improved conditions? It is evident that it must be progressive too, and the responsibility rests upon it to so train up the young that the activity of each individual of future society may be felt as a blessing and not as a curse. In order suitably to educate the young for a future sphere of usefulness, education must not look at a present order of things merely, but must also consider what higher conditions of society these children may be required to meet, when they reach maturity, and for which they need training. Education should not therefore remain stationary, but should be reformed according to the demands of the times. The old landmarks are removed not only in politics, but in science, religion, art, and industry; the limits are extended, the conditions for taking an active part, are heightened; and for every individual, in whatever department of human exertion he may choose his lifework, the requirements are greater and the number of duties increased.

The idea of general culture is scarcely fifty years old, and yet what a change in its requirements! The justice of this demand for general culture in all grades of society is becoming more fully recognized. The common schools in their progressive tendency have acknowledged the rightfulness of the claim on the whole, but have they done all that is needful? Without underrating the importance of improvements made in public instruction, we may put the pertinent question: have all the requirements that the present time has a right to make regarding harmonious, human development been fully met? Have the best of our schools, while imparting a knowledge of what is good, just, noble, beautiful and elevated, sufficient to satisfy the demands of a higher morality, also imparted the power to realize in life that which has been recognized in principle? Are their pupils fitted to enter upon those moral and social reforms that are needed to bring about a better state of society? Alas, facts answer in the negative! Look at the crowded prisons and houses of correction, the numerous hospitals and insane asylums, the increasing number of divorces, the wide spread immorality, the suicides and homicides, the immense increase of pauperism,—in spite of labor and commerce freed from former restrictions, and notwithstanding an enormous advance in the most important branches of industry—and then say what the testimony is in regard to education! Does not irreligion, mocking the highest aspirations of the human soul, itself supported by shallow reasoning and pampering coarse, debasing appetites, increase? In spite of our many churches, are not fraud and corruption rampant everywhere, and are such the fruits of a true, healthful education commensurate with a high state of culture, the boast of our century?

Yet all we have said touches only the outside of existing conditions. What misery is revealed, if we look into the hidden folds of society! Selfishness in its coarsest and most refined forms, meanness of every kind, greed of gain, the barter of principles for money, these are the vices working secretly and claiming to be virtues. Shams of every sort prevail to such an extent that faith in unselfish devotion to principle in good men has almost disappeared, and the best motives of devoted souls are distrusted: they are martyrs doomed to fight against the argument that "this state of things has always been and will be as long as there are men and human passions". Such an assertion merely shows that people have not intelligently and seriously studied the history of human development; for that history shows clearly the difference between the social condition of civilized nations and barbaric hordes and tribes; it shows too how far our culture is in advance of the primitive condition of our forefathers. The really great minds of all times and all nations agree in the belief that the human race is fitted and destined to attain a much higher degree of perfection, and consequently to a state of greater well-being and happiness.

But the solution of this problem, the working out of our destiny, is dependent on the harmonious development of all powers and talents, and on each stage of development it is essential that the degree of intelligence attained be balanced by the degree of morality expressed in life and action. To establish the equilibrium between intelligence and moral power as evinced in the outward life, is in a great measure if not solely the task that Education has now to attempt. The school alone is unable to accomplish it, because it takes into account almost exclusively the intellect, and merely imparts knowledge. But this by itself is not sufficient to prevent or to keep in subordination sin, crime and meanness. If ignorance may be charged with part of the evil, the greater part of it must be attributed to a lack in the cultivation of the heart and conscience, to want of exercise of the moral faculties,— culture which falls chiefly within the province of home, of the family and of society. If it were otherwise, we should not as now find that large numbers of our criminals are intelligent people who have had the advantages of schools. The history of every age shows that a one-sided cultivation of the intellect does not save men from evils of all kinds, and that it even helps them to commit wicked deeds more skilfully. The assertion that crime has diminished in the last century, may be true, but it does not appear that morality has gained on the whole. If the number of open, gross outrages on humanity has been less, yet the sum of more private wrongs, of unjust deeds, of fraud, unblushing selfishness and shame, has greatly increased. Human society bears on its crown the flowers of intelligence, while its roots rot in the swamp of materialism. The enlightened spirit of the age struggles up to the heights of culture, but its feet are fettered with the chains of low sensuality. In the midst of a wide spread but too superficial civilization, individuals everywhere are reaching after conditions which alone can secure their welfare and happiness. The gulf between insight and attainment, between aspiration and accomplishment, between the ideal and the reality, grows wider and wider, as the evils of society are more clearly recognized. The efforts for improvement are too often failures. Let no one accuse us of painting in too dark colors! If we would reform society, we must first reveal existing evils and point out their consequences, not, however, ignoring the good that also exists, or failing to acknowledge at the same time the progress already made in certain directions. God is the same in all ages, and His light shines everywhere!

One of the evils of the present day we find to be the want of a true education, such as is required for a generation sound neither in body nor soul. This youthful generation is perhaps the least happy in many centuries. Precociousness of intellect, love of criticism, of excitement and self-gratification, are not the signs of a healthful, hopeful youth cherishing noble ideals which, realized in manhood, would bring about a purer state of society.

Only new and better men can create better conditions. These men must be the outgrowth of a new and better system of education equal to the demands of our present state of culture. The school must assume part of this work, but only a part, by enlarging its sphere, by incorporating fresh life elements. As all the activities of life make use of, or take advantage of, the discoveries in every branch of science, so the school must include the activities of real life, in order to prepare its pupils to combine theory and practice, thinking and doing. It should no longer be merely a place in which to acquire learning, it ought no longer to teach sciences apart from their application to life, but should prepare the young for the practical everyday work of their existence. Above all it ought to give its pupils opportunity for the exercise of *moral powers*. For this, free activity is requisite; only a *free choice* of the true and good gives to our actions the stamp of a higher morality. The study of historical examples, of elevated thoughts, of noble deeds, does not suffice for a truly moral education; we must furnish a field of action, in which our youth can exercise themselves in noble and generous deeds. Besides this they need conditions favorable to the acquisitions of *good habits* as a basis for all virtues. No one can become a master in any great art by merely committing its theories to memory. Education must furnish more than verbal instruction. The Bible tells us to work and pray; that is, approach in thought, in aspiration, to the Most High, and show forth this spirit of communion in deeds. Mere verbal instruction is, of course, easier for teacher and pupil, but therefore hurtful to the latter. He gets used to a mere reception of facts into the memory without thinking or investigating for himself. But healthy, normal development proceeds differently. The young mind can receive properly only a very limited amount of instruction, can only slowly assimilate and make it its own. It at first only truly receives that which is presented in a tangible, a concrete form. But even in the contemplation of the concrete, of the object, it depends upon the organization of the pupil, whether by his own observation he gains a clear mental image which will make a lasting impression and be wrought into a perception, or whether the image is vague, the impression transient, and so the perception wanting.

The young mind feels, moreover, a desire to reproduce the images and perceptions it has acquired; to embody them in an external, concrete form, in order to make them more definite and clear to itself. This strongly defined need of the child's nature, is suppressed by mere verbal instruction that comes far too early to load the mind through the memory with a burden of facts, weakening and destroying its higher faculties.

It is of the greatest importance to the well-being and happiness of all men, that each one should occupy that place in society, for which he is, by his organization and peculiar talents, best fitted. It is necessary therefore to recognize this natural inner bent at an early period, in order to bring outer conditions into harmony with it. In the realms of nature harmony prevails, because everything is in the place for which it is by its peculiar characteristics adapted; it does not strive to be something or somewhere else. What produces harmony in unconscious nature, must also produce harmony in the world of humanity, if a conscious obedience be rendered to the same law. The only means to secure this obedience and promote this harmony, lie in the recognition, even in childhood, of an inner vocation, for the fulfilment of which Education may then proceed to prepare the child.

Man will and must seek for happiness. He finds it only when, in work, in the fulfilment of duty and general usefulness, he gives expression to his inner life. By no other means can he attain true happiness and contentment. If the way to this can be made smooth from earliest childhood, if education can guide in the right direction, and impart power to fulfil the individual vocation, thousands of missteps may be saved each one who otherwise will blindly follow natural impulse and seek happiness where it is not to be found. Human passions, which always lead astray, can only be counterbalanced by giving the higher aspirations of every human being opportunity for spontaneous expression, by so developing them that under all circumstances they can make their mark. Well-being thus secured through the higher moral powers, through the fulfilment of duties, and of a calling which exercises all the personal, ideal life-elements, is a strong safeguard against temptation to seek happiness in low sensual pleasures. Inner and outer harmony of existence will be thus attained, and strength gained to overcome discords in the conditions of the world.

Every self-conscious man needs a centre, round which his deeds, his desires and aspirations may revolve. The want of such a centre causes discord and unhappiness. The higher this central point is placed, the easier it is to discover the relations of personal activity to the life of the community. This relation of the individual to the community is implied when we speak of a higher morality, of true, exalted contentment.

For man is not a single, unconnected being, but a link in the interminable chain of mankind, closely bound to those who live with him, to those who lived before him, and to all who shall live after him.

At present we have only the semblance of such an expansion of individual existence into that of humanity; we have the assent of intellect but not the response of the heart. A semblance can never truly confer blessings; truth only can do that. But this want of reality causes universal discontent. If we would secure true happiness, education must from the very outset make its conditions possible. These conditions are supplied, when the natural impulses are gratified in an *ideal manner*.

This contentment the child experiences at first through that which is agreeable to him, as in physical sensations; then through the beautiful, in impressions made by external things, and later through that which is good, in the approval of his own conscience. But in order to reach this goal, he must furthermore acquire good habits and self-activity, which beginning in childish play lead on to moral action.

For the supply of conditions favorable to such development, the child is dependent upon the two mighty agents of Education, the family and the school. As yet both fail to give what is required. Education in the family is left to chance, or is dependent on the natural capability and fitness of the parents, the best of whom have no sure guide in their work, and the greater part of whom deal thoughtlessly and arbitrarily with their children. The school, on the other hand, offers only the means for intellectual growth, and cannot therefore act directly on the moral faculties. It lacks means for promoting free activity, for calling forth the ideal in productions of beauty, and for exercising the full powers of its pupils, without which neither the moral faculties nor the individual vocation can be developed and strengthened.

To meet such conditions, a deeper knowledge of the child's nature is needed, a knowledge of its original endowments and capacities, which have at first no definite form, no certain tendency, so that the educator may be enabled to direct them toward the true goal, the good, the beautiful and the true. If we can not do this in absolute perfection, still we may demand of Education that it keep this in view as its end, and that every reform in its systems shall regard the improvement of means for the attainment of this end, this ideal goal.

If the pedagogues of former times have expressed similar thoughts, and have attempted to realize them, yet the present condition of society proves that the means they employed were not, or are no longer, effective. A new genius was needed to add a fresh element to the old, to carry it still higher, and this genius we find in FRIEDRICH FRŒBEL, who was the first to discover the means by which harmony is established between receiving and reproducing, learning and practising, knowing and doing, from the first dawn of conscious life in the child on through all subsequent stages according to their requirements. Here then we have a beginning of the solution of the great educational problem. Education can now proceed in accordance with nature. Body and soul are to be duly cared for, the one is not to be neglected and suppressed for the sake of the other, but the body, by discipline of the senses and cultivation of the natural impulses, is to be raised to an equality with the mind. If perfect union be not immediately attained, at least a more perfect balance will be established in the duality of human nature, and the two forces in it which we have been accustomed to regard as antagonistic, will be brought into harmonious action.

FRŒBEL does not deny that man has inherent tendencies and inclinations to evil, but he thinks that it is the province of Education to turn such tendencies into good channels, so that evil may become less and less. Who can determine the degree in which sin and evil may be eradicated by education? But unless it strive for this, education is without a true and firm basis.

The belief in salvation from sin through Christ is not here touched, for no one thinks that absolute perfection is to be attained by this mode of education; but a new beginning is needed, so that we may by further development come nearer to the realization of Heaven upon earth, or the Kingdom of Heaven within us.

This new beginning must be made in the family at the commencement of the child's life, by its natural educator, the mother. The mother must not be guided solely by instinct, for instinct is blind and does not suffice for the guidance of rational beings. She needs to understand all the child's impulses, in order to satisfy them and give them the means to develop spontaneously and rightly. This science, the true science of mothers, FRŒBEL has put before us. By it the family will be able to exert educational influence, to prepare the soil, and, above all, to develop moral power, a task for which the school alone is not adequate.

No one will deny that education in the early part of a child's life is eminently a woman question; for does not the duty of the early training of the child devolve upon the mother? And if, for some cause or other, the mother is unable to fulfil her duty, is it not to woman again that she has to intrust the charge? But is every one of that sex, in virtue of being a woman, fitted by nature to assume such great responsibilities? or is some previous training required to enable her nobly and conscientiously to fulfil her task, even as a man has to be trained for his avocations in life? Are the ignorant capable of fulfilling this duty as well as those who have deeply and seriously reflected upon the subject, and have tried to make themselves acquainted with all that appertains to the laws of life and health, to the laws of morals and of mind? Do our girls receive an education that fits them for the holy duties of maternity? Would not even the most intellectual mothers, if they were honest, admit that they had made grave mistakes in the education of their children, that they knew very little on the subject when they had the first child? Everybody seems to rely on instinct in this most important matter, ignorant that there is, or ought to be, a *science of education*, with certain laws as fixed as those of every other science where like causes produce like results. Certainly instinct goes a great way in teaching mothers what to do with their offspring, but should rational human beings trust merely to instinct, with which, as we all know, our Creator has not so perfectly endowed the human race as He has animals? Has He not given us reason instead? Is it not self-evident then that we should consult reason, and try to acquire knowledge, on a subject of such vast importance, so closely related to the destiny of the race?

But on looking around us in human society, we must become aware, if we do not blind ourselves to the fact, that our knowledge on this most important point is very limited and crude. If poor helpless children could make an outcry against all the ill-treatment they receive, could protest against the outrages which they suffer, often at the hands of tender but mistaken parents, the world would be startled! As it is, they have to bear their misery in silence as long as they are able, and often by shortened lives or ruined health do they pay the penalty of physical ill-treatment. Not so readily is the perversion of their souls, the stunting of their minds, traced back to earliest causes, as is their physical condition in later years. Yet it is true that the earliest impressions are the most lasting, and that character is formed,—irrespective of ante-natal influences, which, however, are not to be lightly estimated,—in the first years of a child's life. Should we not then greet with joy those good and wise men whom Providence has sent and illuminated in such an important matter as the education of the human race? Should we not be anxious to learn this new science?

Our own country has had men who devoted their lives to the cause of education. Let us hear what HORACE MANN says about physical deterioration: "The present generation is suffering incalculably under an ignorance of physical education. The fifteen millions of the United States, at the present day, are by no means the five times three millions of the revolutionary era. Were this degeneracy attributable to Mother Nature, we should compare her to a fraudulent manufacturer who, having established his name in the market for the excellence of his fabrics, should avail himself of his reputation to palm off subsequent bales or packages with the same stamp, or ear-mark, but of meaner quality. * * * * * The old hearts of oak are gone; society is suffering under a curvature of the spine, and if the deterioration holds out at its present rate, especially in cities, we shall soon be a bed-ridden people." Further he says on the danger of the Republic: "I do not hesitate to affirm that our republican edifice at this time,—in present fact and truth,—is not sustained by those columns of solid and ever-en-during adamant, intelligence and virtue. Its various parts are only just clinging together by that remarkable cohesion,—that mutual bearing and support, which unsound portions of a structure may impart to each other, and which, as every mechanic well knows, will, for a time, hold the rotten materials of an edifice together, although not one of its timbers could support its own weight: and unless, therefore, a new substructure can be placed beneath every buttress and angle of this boasted Temple of Liberty, it will soon totter and fall, and bury all indwellers in its ruins." But of what can this new substructure be formed, save of the children who constitute the coming generation? It is the task of mothers to form their characters.

PESTALOZZI has done a great deal to reform education, and was the first in history who called upon the *mothers* to aid him in his work; he knew well that education consisted not merely in instruction or, even worse, in mere memorizing of facts. He said, "I will make education the basis of the common moral character of the people, and will put the education of the people in the hands of the mothers." And so he did, in giving them the Book for Mothers, or "*How Gertrude teaches her Children.*" If the family is not the holy temple of God, if the mother does not vivify the heart and head of the child, it is in vain to expect a reform in social matters. This was PESTALOZZI'S belief, and it was also that of FRIEDRICH FRŒBEL who devoted his whole life to the study of education, and to the practical embodiment of his ideas on the subject. His system is based so entirely upon the nature of the child and its requirements for development, that, after it is known and applied, people are struck with wonder that all those means which seem so simple and to the purpose, have not long been known and in use. Let us now see what he has to teach us.

Chapter II.

The Child's Being.—Its Relation to Nature, Man, and God.

The child is born; struggling it enters life; a scream is its first manifestation. Its destiny is activity, it has to conquer the world, in whatever social conditions its cradle is placed. A thick veil hangs over its future. The green bud does not disclose what kind of a flower it will develop. Can the mother even guess what destiny is in store for her new-born babe? Can she tell whether he will become a benefactor of humanity or a miserable criminal? May she contribute something toward the former? May she prevent the latter? Who will doubt that she can do something in both these directions? Let us presuppose the natural endowments of a Beethoven, a Washington, a Raphael, a Goethe, and let us place their cradle in a den of misery and vice,—the period of childhood passed without loving care, without guidance, in demoralizing surroundings, youth passed among drunkards, thieves, and murderers,—what natural endowments would have become developed? Almost none. Natural endowment may even be a weapon in the hands of the wicked. Or, if the cradle of such a favored one by nature be placed in the palace of a rich man, and weak and careless parents bring up the child in luxury and idleness,—will, in such a case, the natural endowments ripen into perfection? It is doubtful if they even show stunted blossoms. But let us suppose the contrary. Let a child of but few natural endowments be brought up far from vice and misery, and equally far from enervating luxury and idleness; whose parents fulfil every thing a human being has a right to demand in point of education and development,—will he in this case become an extraordinary being, a great artist, a great character, marking his place in human society? Certainly not. A great genius, or a great character, brings his endowments into the world. You cannot expect roses from thistles. Even the best endowed, educated among all the influences the best methods of education can bring to bear, be it FRŒBEL's method or any other, would he be an absolutely perfect human being? Not so! The inherent evils of our human nature, the imperfection of surrounding circumstances, will still be felt. We are incapable of determining what is due to natural endowment, to surroundings, to education given, to self-education, and to the internal workings of the spirit of God, the Holy Ghost, or the influx of divine life in the regenerated man. But the more we can learn from educational science concerning the being of man, the more we adapt education to its true end,—the more perfectly will the human race develop itself. The being, the capabilities of humanity, have not yet been understood or fully brought out. We have that *one* type of God-man, Christ, as an ideal, as an example set before us. We know that the human race was once made in the image of God, that God is the author of our being; to return to this God-likeness we believe is our destiny, therefore *eternal* progression only is able to solve the problem of that destiny. We do not know what may be, in this state of existence, the degree of progress and development, of which our race is capable. FRŒBEL said: "Man has not received his soul from man"; and he repeats often in his writings: "man is the child of nature, the child of man, and the child of God"; in this threefold character alone can he be understood. By accepting this threefold character of man's being, he solves the opposite of body and spirit by the connecting link of man. Certain it is, that the child with his first breath enters into a threefold relation,—to nature, to man, and to God.

1. As child of nature, man is related to all organisms of creation, and even to the inorganic, the earthy particles of which (in the bones for instance) may be traced in his organism. As a product of the earth, he is not only subject to its laws, but he lives on it, he exists by it, he proceeds from it, and returns to it. The earth is his mother: as a seed it bore the human race in its bosom, like all other seeds of creation. He is surrounded by its atmosphere, out of it his natural life ceases. Climate and soil, food and raiment, mode of life, imprint the stamp of races and people, of which

the individual man is an ingredient. There is no product in nature that does not enter into intimate relations with the human being. Everywhere is interchange of matter between man and nature, and man ending his earthly career leaves to earth his bodily covering, which resolves into earth. By nature men are solidarily connected, each generation with itself, and all generations with each other; for, from the first to the last, the great chemistry of the world has remodelled them, as well as all other natural objects. There is but *one* law in creation, and it rules the heavenly bodies as well as the worm, the animal, and man; for their originator, their creator, is one and the same—God. And because a spirit, the divine, lives in nature as well as in the soul of man, man is capable of comprehending nature. We have only arrived at the symbolism of nature; with bold steps Science conquers in our day one realm after another. If we place again the young generation, from its cradle, under the mighty influence of God's creation, so that its intuitive language may take hold on its soul and awaken an echo, mankind will soon explore the secrets which are the key of all life, and the hieroglyphics of this symbolism will soon be deciphered by all.

2. But, as the child of man, the young citizen steps out of the circle of necessity into the realm of freedom, of self-consciousness. The stamp of the natural being is simple, easily recognized, the individual is the reflection of the species. But, as a human being, the right to an individuality as a personality begins,—a

personality which, once gained, is not lost, but leads on in the chain of self-conscious beings whose highest link is with God.

Who may unravel the thousand-threaded web of descent? Who can tell what is due to the race, to the nation, to the family, or to the individual? Do not all the traits of the ancestors live in the descendants, either developed or dormant? No one can wholly sever the chain of which he is a link. Nobody can withdraw from the inheritance of his fathers, whether it consist in features, in motions, or in peculiarities of his soul, in good or bad qualities. It is true that the sins of the fathers will be visited upon the children unto the fourth generation, but the same is true of virtues; and the free will of each individuality may, by overcoming, decrease the amount of sin and increase the amount of virtue. The moral advance of the race consists in this: that each individual may increase the talent inherited from a previous generation, and leave it with accumulated interest to the following one.

Retrogressions, by individuals as well as families and nations, are inevitable in the great school of experience, in which Providence has placed mankind. But to deny progress in the mass, and on the whole, is denying Providence itself, who has placed the longing for something better, even in earthly conditions, in the soul of man, and based his whole mental and moral development on it. Without accepting the capacity for improvement and progression in the individual and in the race, education would have no basis. Humanity is a whole; it is destined to develop itself as one organism, and to manifest itself as such, by the conscious connection of its links, by the brotherhood of man which all religions teach. Therefore the individual can only be comprehended as a part of the species, and the species can only be understood through a knowledge of peculiar individual traits. The more exactly and completely the individual character manifests itself, the nearer it will come to the universal development of the human race. Harmony in music is only attained, when each individual instrument expresses its peculiar sound perfectly.

On the connection of single individuals among themselves, and their relation to past, present, and future generations, rests the shadow of darkness; but with the progress of all science, the science of mankind advances. The time will come, when humanity shall have attained what philosophers of all ages have pointed out as the very essence of wisdom—self-knowledge; when it shall have made practical the precept: "know thyself"! All knowledge must pass from the easier to the more difficult; so the road to man's self-knowledge leads first through all the organisms of nature below him. He has to look at himself first through the mirror of natural objects, till he recognizes himself in his own mirror as a human being.

Only in the reflection of his race, in the history of mankind, man sees what he is in his kind, if even now only in fragments. Different as the epochs are, much as nations, or much as individuals, differ from one another, the universal, common traits of humanity are reflected for each one of us from the history of the race. What is it that gives immortality to the dramas of Shakespeare? It is his delineation of the grand traits of a common humanity in such a characteristic, individual manner. The common traits of humanity are eternally the same, and will be understood at all times, in all forms.

The human race experienced and experiences, as the individual does, from its birth, the different grades of development: infancy, youth, manhood and the culmination of development. And again, in the development of the life of the individual, the general traits belonging to the development of the race, as we trace it in history, may be seen.

It is FRŒBEL's undenied merit to have recognized this fact, and to have found the means to aid in this development from earliest infancy.

In the instinctive manifestations of the child's being, if not interfered with by artificial drill, there appear traces of the road that humanity has travelled from the beginning of civilization. The instinct of the animal is strong enough at the outset to provide for the means of its existence. The animal races have not changed their functions: the bee fashions its cell, the swallow builds its nest, the fox has its den now as ever before. Man alone, from the first rude life in nature, by toil and exertion, aided by his powerful inventive genius, has forced his way through a thousand errors and false steps, up to his present height of civilization. The history of culture shows what man is, and what has been attained by him; the future will show what he can do, and what there may yet be for him to accomplish. But whatever production emanates from the human mind, whether it be the ancient rude tools made of stones and roots, or the most ingenious machinery of modern times; whether it be the rude outline and drawing of the shadows of objects, or the wonderful works in painting and sculpture; whether it be the uncouth imitations, by the forest savage, of birds and the different sounds in nature, or the grand and sublime symphonies of Beethoven; whether it be the knowledge of the relations of space and size obtained by the first rectangle measured, or through the measurement of the heavenly bodies by modern science, Nature's laws still guide and govern all man's formations, and gauge his endeavors. Man could and can only create after the models of his Creator; they were his patterns, and man's creations are ennobled by the stamp of genius and art. They became symbols of truth to him, visible signs of the Invisible, until he was capable of understanding immediate revelation. In soft, imperceptible gradations, from the rudest and most simple in sensuous perception to the expression of divine beauty in works of art, and of truth in the Word, God, the sublime Educator, leads His human children.

In the plays of children of all times, the being of humanity is expressed. As an indistinct remembrance and presentiment, the past and future of its life float through the soul of the child, and groping it tries to take hold of the thread, from within and without, which is to guide it through the labyrinth, and help it to accomplish its destiny.

As the birds build nests, and men first provide themselves with shelter, so the children of men build houses or caverns in their play. As the chickens scratch in the earth, and men early in their career on earth begin to cultivate the soil, so little children love to dig the ground in their play, and learn in a little garden how to cultivate the soil, to sow and reap. All material in their hands, if it be only moist sand, serves for plastic formations. Every art will be attempted by the child, whether it be to make forms with chalk or pencil, or to delineate them in sand, whether it be the inarticulate sounds of the babe trying to become rhythmic or to imitate the crowing of the cock, the lowing of the cow or the barking of the dog, until at length real musical sounds proceed from the throats of little children. These early attempts are the first beginnings of development in art. As the first elements of art and industry show themselves in the activity of children, so likewise the germs of science are exhibited in the desire for knowledge. With its always repeated questions,—why? wherefore? whence? the young mind searches for the cause of all things, for truth and its source—God.

It is an internal necessity that the development of individuals should pass through the same phases as that of all humanity, because their destiny is the same —happiness; or, according to FRŒBEL, "joy, peace, and freedom", are what the individual as well as humanity strives for. It can be attained only by full development of the whole of the human being. True education is the principal means to this end, but this means can only become available through a true knowledge of man. It is only by this knowledge that the secret of human destiny will be made known.

Each human being is a peculiar thought of God, in that which is his spiritual originality. The child of God lives in man as only a faint spark when he enters this world. The human existence serves to nurse it into a flame. In the beginning, the child of nature predominates as instinctive life: as an impulse that awakens the will, which at first is an ungoverned power of nature. Self-preservation is the unconscious aim of all the child's first manifestations. We ought not to blame the child for its so-called selfishness. If an all-wise Providence had not put this impulse, so strong and powerful, in the human breast, how could such weak, helpless creatures maintain their existence among innumerable dangers? But education has to modify and moderate this impulse of self-preservation, and lead the child to practically exercise its capacity to love, and thus guide it out of the narrow circle of its own personality into the character of the child of man, the social being, a link of humanity. In this sphere feeling predominates, and intellect begins to guide the will-power, and show it a higher aim than individual well-being alone.

Self-reliance, independence, freedom are the highest expressions of the human being as an individual. How backward would be the development of the world, if it were not for the innate, inborn impulse that actuates men to obtain an independent, distinguished position in the world! Almost all progress is due to the fact that each one wants to be himself the centre of activity; and this desire urges him on to a thousand exertions, to countless inventions, to a continuous change of his position, and, therefore, of all existence.

3. But as long as man thinks only of himself, even in the widened circle of his family relations, so long the child of God slumbers in him. It only awakens and springs to life, when love, which at first comprised only self and the narrow circle of a few in the generation, drives him forth into the larger community of the people; then this love becomes strong in him, without self-reference; he devotes himself, even though he sacrifices his own earthly personality, to the service of the whole. Whosoever serves humanity serves God. The words, "He that loveth not his brother, how can he love God?" indicate the essence of all religion. Only the child of God, with consciousness of this aim, is truly religious. By love, out of our own personality, we come into the love of God, in the higher community which exists beyond this visible world. By each ideal aspiration we overstep the boundaries of this temporal, visible life, and enter a world in which

the mortal becomes immortal. If everywhere in the universe an uninterrupted connection exists, by death only a *seeming* discontinuance can take place. The image of God, which man is destined to become, cannot be confined within the narrow limits of this sphere; man, as such, becomes a citizen of the universe which, in gradual changes, he traverses, and overcomes both space and time. Who will deny that man's destiny is to be in community with God, and at last in unity with Him?

Did ever a true human being, a man who merited the name by his own development, go through his earthly career, without knowing the longing for something higher and better than this world can bestow? Did he not feel, in a moment of great agitation, whether of joy or of pain, that there was something beyond the limits of this existence? Is any work of man, even the highest; any action, even the greatest to be conceived, that would not presuppose something higher, something better? Nowhere are full contentment and satisfaction in human existence; everywhere presentiment, longing, hope, reaches out beyond it to the ideal of man,—as it once was presented to us in Him who gave his life for his brethren,—toward the spring of all fullness and perfection, toward God.

He is the child of God, who enters into the higher freedom, because he has learned to feel the higher love. Only through love is liberty possible; for it overcomes that which is a hinderance to liberty. No laws of restraint are needed for those who would never violate them, and only he who is possessed of perfect freedom, can give himself in perfect love. All great benefactors of humanity, all true heroes, all martyrs, all saints, all real artists, all great explorers in truth and science, as well as all humble souls who have lived in childlike trust and piety, have been children of God. In them the divine spark flames as enthusiasm which cleanses and purifies the human soul, and permits it to be penetrated by the spirit of God.

It matters little whether you circumscribe or exalt the degree of attainable perfection here on earth. If progress is once accepted as the eternal law, it must lead to higher aims. There are but two alternatives: either earth is a treadmill in which humanity continually circulates without proceeding farther, or humanity is destined to attain even on earth a certain God-appointed goal, which leads on farther into the great hierarchy of the universe.

If all believed in this high destiny, if they knew that *all*, all without exception, according to God's will, had to work to attain this end, how much quicker would it be attained! How much more easily would pain and misery be endured and overcome, were we to keep in view the great end: that for its attainment each experience must be undergone, that each pain must be suffered and its cause removed, before sufferer and worker can finally share in the glory of that attainment! This is the true belief, the belief of the glorification of God in mankind, this is the belief that all religions have to presuppose; it is the essence of christianity; and one of the reasons why our generation has so little religion, is because this faith is wanting! So long as it is deemed an Utopian dream to believe in this apotheosis of humanity, so long it will remain unrealized.

But the victory of the child of God cannot be attained, if the child of nature, or the child of man, is suppressed or strangled. The true accord of man's being appears only then, when each chord has its full force and value; when the higher nature elevates the others to equal perfection.

Education can only fulfil its mission, when it views the human being in this threefold relation, and takes each into due account. Education could not fulfil this mission till now, not only because the child's being was so little understood, but because the means were wanting to supply the demands of the young soul from the beginning. FRŒBEL found the key to unlock the child's being, he understood its natural mute language; he found also the means to give it its first soul nourishment, and to treat the child, from its entrance into life, as a reasonable being endowed with a high destiny.

But where shall we find mothers to accept this rich bequest from the educational genius of our time, and to employ it in the right manner? Let us look into all grades of society and see how many women we can count who are truly mothers and educators. And even the best of these lack the knowledge and means to accomplish this end.

The true science of mothers has been founded by

FRŒBEL, to strike at the root of the awful corruption in matters of education, and thereby to prevent intense misery of all kinds.

With the true recognition of the child's being, the elevation of the female sex is closely connected. The science of mothers introduces woman into a higher knowledge; not the stimulation of dry, intellectual attainments, but the development of true feeling, genuine wisdom. With the consciousness, that a divine spark glows in the little being on her lap, enthusiasm will be kindled in her to nurse it, and to educate a true citizen of Heaven. With this consecration of woman as the educator of the human race, everything is connected that elevates her to the true dignity of humanity.

Chapter III.

The Child's Manifestations.

Not Frœbel alone, but other thinkers of the present day and of former times, have expressed the thought, that the individual can only develop according to its species, and that this fact should guide us in its education and treatment. Frœbel founded his Kindergartens on this truth. Now let us see whether his means are really adapted to the end.

What are the principal manifestations of the child? They are those which are more or less common to *all* children, and in which the beginnings of the efforts of the human race after culture may be seen. When the child is born, its first manifestation is *motion*, motion of its limbs, motion of its interior by screaming: development can only come by motion. Before the human being can begin to take possession of himself and of the world outside of himself, his bodily powers and organs must be somewhat developed; therefore *bodily development* is chief in the first years of his life. The child a few months old, lying in its cradle, plays with its limbs, grasps its tiny feet, kicks, plays with its fingers. In this way it learns about its own form. The child's greatest desire, when it is able to walk, is again motion; to run to and fro,—in much the same way as a little dog,—to go in all directions, to touch and take hold of everything with the hands, to be always in motion, is characteristic of every healthy child. The more its strength increases, the greater the necessity for exertion of all kinds, that drives the boy, especially, to games of running, climbing, jumping, throwing, lifting, which require strength and skill. The child itself, however, has not this end in view, it is merely driven by its impulse, the gratification of which gives it pleasure. *What gives pleasure to children generally and in all times, serves always for their development in some way:* therefore physical development is the unconscious aim of all activity in early childhood.

Physical exertions and training, chiefly for the sake of procuring the means of sustenance, characterize the life of savages, and were the prominent features in that of the uncultivated peoples of former ages. The first authenticated records of history, including the heroic age, show that while the development of physical strength and dexterity was still predominant, heroic action served other than purely material and egotistical purposes; it was often dictated by friendship or love of country. Exertion of strength, conquest of obstacles or foes, are always the greatest pleasures of youth and early manhood. Even in the middle ages, tournaments, duels, and the chase, alternated almost like play with the sterner occupation of war. Nothing shows more clearly that physical development was the highest pleasure of the human race, in the period of its childhood, than the mythology of the northern peoples. They believed that the dead divide their life in Valhalla, or their Heaven, between combats and feasts, but with the advantage that wounds received in combat heal immediately, and those who are killed are quickly able to sit at the festive board.

The limbs and organs of the body must be developed to a certain degree, before they can serve as adequate tools for the mind. We see clearly how Divine Providence always incites each being to do that which serves for its development. The child is not obliged, as man was in his primitive state, to procure its physical sustenance; but it is moved by inner impulse to use its limbs and organs in play, so that they develop. But it is not safe to leave the impulses of human beings to themselves; they are apt to degenerate, and to lead to what we call evil, and so to lead away from their purpose which is development. Education of a child is furthering its natural manifestations in such a way that nature's aims are attained, always bearing in mind the child's threefold relation. There is so much less demand in our time for great exertion of strength, so much less effort needed to overcome external obstacles, that we have, like the Greeks, to employ gymnastics of various kinds in the physical education of youth, although these are not so generally used as they should be. To meet the demands of the impulses of childhood in this respect, very little is done, where FRŒBEL's Kindergartens are not introduced. Gymnastics and games are the fulfilment of the first impulses of childhood toward development.

After the development of rude force, that of the skill of the hand became foremost as the principal condition for the beginnings of human industry. The word "handeln", to act, in German is derived from the member chief in action—the hand. In English "to handle" is somewhat equivalent. The great desire in early infancy,—second only to the craving for motion in general,—is to use the hands. The sense of feeling is,—next to that of tasting, which is also a feeling of the tongue,—predominant in the first development of the senses. In the beginning of life all the senses are, as it were, somewhat united. The little effort of which each is capable, necessitates the common action of all. Children, as well as grown persons of little cultivation, naturally wish to touch everything they see; the eye alone does not suffice to give them cognizance of an object.

In order that the chief instrument for work, the hand, be well prepared, nature prompts the child to use its hands constantly in play. Nothing is more contrary to nature than to forbid a child the use of its hands, yet this is always done in schools. That children may pay attention to the subject taught, they are required to fold their hands, or to cross them on the back. But FRŒBEL has followed the hint of nature, has found *means to chain the child's attention, by connecting all instruction given with the use of its hands.* The hand is the natural sceptre which Providence has given man as king of the earth. With his hands, man procured all defensive weapons possessed naturally by animals but denied to him. Through the work of his hands, he obtained all the tools with which to conquer the forces of nature and matter, and to procure the necessaries and embellishments of life. Without the development of skill in the hand, industry and art are impossible. But the wonders of industry and art are not due solely to the remarkable construction of this member; indeed man's activity is *work* in its true sense, only when the *mind* guides the fingers which merely serve to carry out its plans and combinations. Work, therefore, is no *curse*, but man's high prerogative. The plays of children are to them like work, serving to develop their limbs, organs and senses. After the first unguided attempts to touch or grasp things, their main delight is to handle some soft mass, be it earth, sand, or even the mud in the street. One of the first impulses of childhood is toward plastic forming; but this impulse does not serve the purpose intended, if education does not undertake, as in the Kindergarten, to provide adequate material, and direct the moulding, in order to bring the awakened instinct into activity for a definite purpose.

The first and easiest forming, after modelling in sand and clay, is building. After the child has dug holes in a sand hill, it proceeds to build houses or whatever its fancy may suggest, and thus its endeavors tend to the creation of an industry on a small scale. The never fading interest of all children in the story of Robinson Crusoe, lies chiefly in the minute description of the efforts made, by a single individual, after culture, a description in which children see their own endeavors reflected as in a mirror. Undoubtedly one of the first attempts of the human race, after caverns in rocks or huts of boughs in the forest were deemed insufficient, was to build dwellings. But when, by improvement in implements of labor, work advanced from its first rough outlines, the combinations of the mind became more manifold, forms more developed; and a sense of the beautiful awakened in our progenitors, as it also awakens in the child. All things shining and brilliant in color, give gladness and joy to children, as they still do to savages. They strive to produce something beautiful in their works, and, by degrees, aim at harmony and symmetry. Children, therefore, not only instinctively delight in modelling and forming, but they also attempt drawing and coloring.

The child sees first the contour of things. Those who have observed children must have noticed them tracing outlines with their fingers, and attempting to draw chairs, tables, houses, or the contour of their own hands on the slate, straight lines always striking the eye before curves. The same is true of the people who earliest attempted architecture—the Egyptians. Their drawings consist of contours,—linear drawings without curves or arches, and without perspective, like the first attempts of the child.

Before the child talks, it produces various sounds; and the instinctive perception of its craving for the rhythmic has taught mothers and nurses the numberless cradle-songs and lullabies with which they accompany the measured swaying and rocking of babes in their arms. The power to distinguish between sounds is among the earliest manifestations of children (how quickly an infant knows its mother's voice!), and instruction in singing is a powerful means of education. Savages and children show a natural desire for singing and dancing,—rhythm of sound, and rhythm of motion.

Even before a child has attempted any productions in art, we have seen it strongly influenced by nature; animals and flowers have fixed its attention. Infants stretch out their arms in delight, when the hat and cloak are brought preparatory to a walk; they are not only pleased to be in the enlivening fresh air, but made happy by the impressions received from the various forms of natural objects.

After children have obtained free use of their limbs, we see all that are not kept from it by parents who fear the soiling of hands and clothes, digging in the earth, — in the garden it may be. At first the nearest stick, or a shovel picked up somewhere, serves as a tool, and they throw up the ground, make hills, and build walls as mere exercise. But, after a little, observation is added to these instinctive manifestations.

the impulse awakens to *cultivate* the earth; to use in play the productivity of the soil for self-benefit: so mankind in its early development used it to obtain a fuller supply and better quality of food. May it not be an undefined idea of the limitation of space, that leads the child to fence its little garden-plot with sticks? The motive that led originally to the cultivation of the soil, was certainly the desire for possession. Without possessions, without property, the individuality of man would never have been so fully developed. Property expands personality by giving a man power to work, means to carry out his will; and, at the same time, it enables him to share what is peculiarly his with others,—to prepare the soil out of love to his neighbor.

But for agriculture man would never have forsaken nomadic life, never have founded cities and communities, never have become a nation, never have known love of country. To many it may seem ridiculous to connect the first small possession of a child with love of country, and see in it the very germ of patriotism. Still, in the nature of things, that which is characteristic of man's life, in greater or less degree, must have an almost imperceptible beginning as the germinating point for development. The largest tree started from a very small seed; and the greatest deeds of man are but the developed emotions of an infant's soul. The love of one's own fireside, is it not the starting point of the love of one's country?

If physical wants first impelled man to cultivate the

soil, it is evident, in the course of history, that a higher motive was soon added, which tended to elevate his soul. The culture of that which serves merely to supply material needs will awaken affection; whatever man takes care of, whatever he works for, that object he loves. We should regard a child that showed no affection for any plaything or pet, as unnatural and degenerate. The little girl attributes to her doll, or the boy to his toy horse, all the feelings of a living being, and loves it accordingly. From these inanimate things, the affections are transferred to domestic animals, or to the flowers of the garden. The child who has never owned a little piece of land, never worked it in the sweat of his brow, never taken loving care of plants and animals, will always have a blank in the development of his soul; he will never have the perfect gift of taking care of human beings. All care and nursing demand the overcoming of indolence, and self-abnegation, which can be acquired only by practice. FRŒBEL suggests that early practical lessons of this kind may be given: let children from their own pocket-money buy food for canary birds, or other pets, and so learn to feel themselves immediately responsible for their care and support. By cultivation of its soil, man established his right to the globe he inhabits; and the first doctrine, in his code of laws, is that duties and rights should be *equal*.

After the child has obtained the use of its limbs and senses; when its activity and observation somewhat awakened have led it into many little experiences, then the impulse to know (sometimes called curiosity) becomes strong: it asks for the cause of things and appearances, incessantly repeating: whence? why? wherefore? The visible world had to furnish material for its perceptions, before the world of thought was roused from slumber. For the sake of obtaining knowledge, the child makes experiments. It knocks different objects together, throws them down, investigates the density of materials, tastes, tears, destroys, in order to ascertain something about their internal structure, and makes a thousand experiments to become acquainted with the quality and the use of things. This process of observation and investigation, is followed by comparison of things among themselves; comparison leads to perception of size, form, color, number, etc. What child does not measure the length and breadth of different objects, to find out which of the two is larger? What child does not like to count the things with which it is occupied, and ask the name and use of each? Alas! the answers given to the child thirsting for knowledge, are often empty words little calculated to satisfy it. No mere words, unaccompanied with demonstrations, can give replies that will be clear to the childish perception. Object lessons should begin with the first plays, not with the first school. How the child's eyes glisten at the discovery of a shining pebble in the road, a new flower in the meadow! It experiences a delight similar to that which the philosopher feels in the discovery of what he believes to be a new truth.

As, in the first awakening of its mind, the child is occupied in finding out how far or how near an object is, or, in other words, with the relations of space, so the knowledge of mankind began with the first elements of mathematics or geometry. The only book open to man in the beginning of his development, was the book of nature; observation and imitation led him from discovery to discovery, each widened the horizon of the mind—increased knowledge. With a knowledge of nature,—at first shallow and superficial as based on mere appearance,—began the intellectual development of mankind. A child's first lessons should likewise be from natural objects. The first abstractions from man's experimental knowledge necessarily led to mathematical conclusions: calculation and conclusion follow comparison. Things are clearly perceived by the understanding, only when they are classified according to number and size.

The child gains its first geographical knowledge from explorations in the playground, the garden or the village; in the same manner, the first geographical notions of mankind were derived from the exploration of neighboring countries, and observation of their climate, soil, products, etc.

With the lives of the Patriarchs,—most interesting to us as Christians,—and those of ancient peoples, history began; its earliest form was oral tradition. What is more interesting to children than stories of what happened in the family before they were in existence? How unweariedly they listen to the grandmother's tales concerning her own young days, or those of her children. The discovery that she is speaking of *their* father or mother when a *little child*, gives deepest interest to the narrative. FRŒBEL would have all families preserve records that might serve in this way as a foundation for further historical knowledge.

All the stages of development we have contemplated man could attain only in connection with his fellow man, by social union. The desire for society we see even in animals; it is more predominant in animals of the higher than of the lower order, and is most deeply rooted in the human being; it is the origin and means of all culture. Solitary confinement is man's worst and most cruel punishment. Very little can be accomplished single-handed; only by associated effort does man overcome space and time; by it he presses natural forces into his service, and so becomes more and more the lord of creation.

The child manifests even in the first months of its life a desire for society; it cries in its cradle if it fancies itself alone, and is often quieted by a single word. But it not only craves the society of grown people, it desires to be with its equals in age and development. Look at the beautiful smile, the happy expression of the eyes, when the smallest child sees children of its own age! One that grows up entirely among older people, will never have the freshness and vivacity which result from a life in community with children; seriousness, sometimes sadness, marks the features of such a one. We have said that social union is the basis of all culture; the play of children among themselves is especially the basis of all moral culture. Without charity, without the various relations between man and man, morals and culture vanish; the desire for society is at the foundation of Church and State, and of all that makes human life what it is.

FRŒBEL thinks, that the first manifestation of religious aspiration, is the child's desire for the society of grown people; it wants somebody to look up to, and may have an undefined feeling that some common object unites all, some common interest binds all together. Let several people assemble in the street, children run to join them, and they even submit to great restraint, for the sake of being in the company of men and women. Their desire to go to church, is based upon this feeling, rather than on one of interest in what goes on there, which is beyond the childish comprehension. The reverent acts of others, their elders, affect them. Certainly this is the first undefined feeling which animates a child's heart; and connected with it is love to its fellows, always preceding love to God. Only through love to mother, father, brethren, is the young soul led to its Heavenly Father. Developed natural affections kindle the sacred flame of religion. Religious feeling or perception, *like every other, is, in its beginning, instinctive.*

In the infant watching the motion of a suspended ball, and following with its eyes along the string from the ball to the hand that guides it, FRŒBEL sees a manifestation of the mind's impulse to seek and find the cause of all effects. This may seem absurd to those who do not admit a psychological reason for the child's manifestations, but that all *conscious* manifestations proceed from the unconscious, no thinker will deny. This being admitted, FRŒBEL's idea is vindicated, that the conception of the mature mind originates in the spontaneity of the child's soul, which awakened by outward appearances, first manifests itself as instinct, or inclination. Hence, he argues, the propriety of beginning instruction with the concrete,—the object which the child can comprehend—, and proceeding very gradually to the abstract thought. He says: that passing from the object to the image or picture, from the picture to the sign, from the sign to the idea, the road leads to consciousness or knowledge. PESTALOZZI expresses a similar opinion in the words: "There is nothing in the mind, that has not passed through the senses". Trace written language back to its beginning. Rude hieroglyphics served at first to convey notions of single objects or events; then a continuous story was given by a series of the same symbols; but not until civilization was far advanced, did abstract thought find expression in arbitrary signs, or alphabetical characters. The science of numbers also begins with the numeration of objects; and the wisdom of illustrating the text of elementary school books with pictures of things to be named or counted, is apparent. Returning to the process of religious development, we find it to be in nowise exceptional. Man's conceptions of a higher, a supreme Being, were gained originally through impressions received from the natural and visible world, even as the child's are now. Man felt his impotence in the presence of the ever-active, gigantic forces of nature, and bowed trembling before their unknown ruler. He found himself, his very existence, dependent on the gifts and benefactions of nature, and when, like a tender mother, she showered bounties upon him, he loved her. Her different aspects gave him the idea of good and evil deities. He worshipped nature in symbols derived from her own treasury, until becoming more conscious of himself and his being, he humanized, as it were, the soul of nature and worshipped it ideally in his gods. The beautiful statues of Greece represented deities that were believed really to exist, and, transcending the idols of other pagan nations, were often personifications of virtues and abstract qualities of the mind.

"Who made all the trees, the flowers, the birds, the little lambs? Who made me? Who made father and mother?" the child asks, seeking the first cause with the natural impulse of a thinking being. Like the savage it is terrified by the rolling thunder which rouses a perception of a higher power; spring's balmy breezes fill it with undefined delight; it anticipates the unseen benefactor who is, as yet, represented to it in the visible presence of its parents. It sits on the grass, in summer time, under a blooming tree on which birds sing sweet songs; fragrant flowers fill its lap, the bright sunshine gladdens all things, and a light warm breeze floats the blossoms from the tree like pure snow flakes against the child's cheek. A sensation of awe and never before experienced bliss, fills its soul,—it whispers: "that is God who is passing by",—and a first revelation of God has entered the soul. Thus, as FRŒBEL says, with natural religion all religion begins; God in man, God as revealed to us in Christ, must also be recognized, but such recognition can only be after God in nature has been felt. On account of these views, FRŒBEL has been attacked by the ultra orthodox, and his system denounced as irreligious. It must be clear to the unprejudiced, however, that, instead of lacking religion, FRŒBEL's method aims to make it a vital necessity, and while guarding the child from the abstract teachings of theology, to nurse and healthily develop the divine spark, so "that body, soul and spirit" may grow harmoniously into the stature of the perfect man.

We see then that the manifestations of *all* children are similar; having the same origin, being founded on natural, inborn impulses, they must be like. But nature does nothing in vain, nothing without a purpose; all natural impulses must therefore tend to something, and can have no other design than to serve for the development of the individual organism. The child plays, it *must* play in order to develop. Its play is its work, destined to awaken its powers and capacities, to train them, to strengthen them, so that it may be fitted to accomplish its destiny as a human being—to become a child of God. The sum of the activities of the human race,—manifested in past and present states of culture,—can likewise only have the purpose to further the development of the human race, as such, by unfolding all its capabilities, and making it what God destined it to be. But as the human race consists of single individuals, the end of individual existence must be the same as that of the community of which it is a part; that end is perfection, not absolute but relative; the perfection of the finite, not of the Infinite.

No one denies that the individual plant, the individual animal, develops according to its species. Only because it is known how the species of the plant, or the race of the animal develops, is the proper mode of nursing or rearing the individual known. According to the modifications of the treatment demanded by nature, according as her laws are complied with or violated, so individual character develops. This is strikingly shown in the case of domestic animals; though of the same race, one is docile, faithful and affectionate, another cross, snappish and obstinate, according to the treatment received.

We have seen then, first: that the manifestations of each being bear the impress of the species to which it belongs, and that man forms no exception; second: that the instinctive, unpremeditated manifestations, common to all individuals of the same species, serve the end of their development. The savage impelled by inner impulse, and influenced by outer attraction, exerts himself to supply his bodily necessities—to maintain existence, and make it comfortable according to his notion of comfort; the child, from like impulse and attraction, plays, and works in play; but both are unconscious that the end served by their exertions, is their development. The history of the culture of the human race, shows us that in the endeavor to satisfy physical wants, to obtain food, raiment, protection from storms and wild beasts, and, later, in the effort to satisfy spiritual desires, in social intercourse, in communication of truth, and in seeking expression for the beautiful, man was led to invent all that is now ours in the departments of industry, art and science. As, in the stage of unconsciousness, man was prepared for the succeeding one of higher development and culture, which, in its turn, led to self-consciousness and a recognition of its destiny, so, in like manner, the playful activity of the child should serve to prepare it for its subsequent conscious personality. This is only attained when the childish groping and attempting are regulated, and when *education* furnishes the *means*. To do this is the design of FRŒBEL's Kindergarten. In it he intended to have children pass through the same stages of development, on a small scale, that have marked the development of the human race, and so gain similar experiences to fit them for future life work, for self-consciousness and a comprehension of the great problem of existence.

Chapter IV.

The Child's Education.

Education is deliverance, deliverance of the fettered forces of body and mind. The inner conditions for this deliverance every healthy child brings into the world. The outer conditions must be supplied by education. In spring time, in order that the hard outer coverings of the buds may burst, and the germs of leaves and flowers be set free and expand, air, sunshine, rain and dew must be allowed them. The inner germinal force bursts the coverings, if outer conditions are favorable. In nature, a need always brings its supply, and the processes of nature without arbitrariness are according to rules and laws. In a plant, the flow of the sap, as it regularly ascends and descends from roots to crown, and crown to roots, by contraction and expansion, forming knotty and intricate points, resembles the circulation of the blood in animal and human organisms, proceeding, as it does, from the heart, returning to the heart, and representing contraction and expansion through the action of the lungs.

In the different realms of nature, everything obeys

an eternal, universal law, and development is synonymous with lawfulness; it is progress according to laws, progress from the formless to the formed, from undevelopment to development. Mental and spiritual, as well as bodily development, must proceed according to law, otherwise education would be impossible. For we call the influence we bring to bear upon the development of the child, to regulate it, to guide it intellectually and morally as well as physically, education; and how can that which proceeds without order or law; that which is arbitrary and incalculable in its manifestations, be regulated and guided? Must not, therefore, the spiritual, or soul development, follow a lawful circuit, similar to the organic circulation, for certainly the organs and the mind which they serve, are in relation as cause and effect? Psychology has discovered the laws of the soul's development, as physiology has discovered the laws of the circulation of the blood; but the former has occupied itself chiefly with the already formed souls of grown persons, that have, by self-determination and deviation from the lawful and normal state, fallen into a certain degree of arbitrariness, the abnormal condition that we name evil; for as the violation of physical laws causes disease, so the violation of moral laws causes moral evil or sin. Wrong culture has demoralized man, and the intentions of the Creator concerning him have not been rightly understood. FRŒBEL said: "If you wish to study the laws of nature, in plants for instance, you must study the simple, the wild plants, commonly called weeds, in preference to cultivated ones with all their complications." From this we must not infer that man should be left in his primitive, uncultured state, but that the human soul is to be studied in its simplicity. The young human plant, in its instinctive, primitive state, uncalculating, unspoiled by false culture, presents to the observer who is capable of seeing and understanding them, the laws and the logical processes of development despite individual differences.

We have seen already that certain manifestations are *common* to *all* children, and that thus the species is marked in each individual. Through such common manifestations, we find a basis for the recognition of the laws of childish development, inasmuch as these traits are repeated in each individual, and are therefore a rule. FRŒBEL says, there is perfect connection in human life, as there is entire harmony everywhere in nature. Certainly we cannot err in saying that the eternal lawfulness which lives in the universe, must also determine the development of the human soul. The educator whose office it is to carry light or warmth, rain or dew, to the human bud in the right manner, that it may be incited to free itself from bondage, and by development and expansion of all its slumbering faculties and powers to produce finally the rare blossom of self-consciousness,—such a one must not only know the laws of development, but he must possess and apply the means to attain this result. His mode of education must be a lawful process like that of nature; it must be *methodical* with a correspondence in its outward means.

It will not be disputed that instruction deserves the name only when it is methodical. Instruction is but a branch of education, and it is evident that the tree must have the same root and ground as the branch. Much as has been done, from antiquity up to our own time, to improve education and instruction; much as has been accomplished even, in adapting methods of instruction to natural development, and in obtaining knowledge by the easiest and best ways,—still the laws of childish intellectual development have hitherto been wrapped in darkness. The magnet unerringly shows the mariner how to guide his ship over the ocean, according to its individual destination, but no such safe guide has been found for the educator, in his work of guiding individual character toward its true end. So long as no firm, unswerving educational method is known, every kind, even the best, seems merely arbitrary, or at hap-hazard. PESTALOZZI's principal aim was to find and apply what he called, "the principle of the organic", to bring instruction into harmony with nature. Whatever knowledge we have gained hitherto of the mode of childish development, we owe to him and his predecessors, as well as some of the means of applying their principle. But for them, FRŒBEL might not have worked out his method, as their conclusions were his starting point, and their hints and practical endeavors he carried on toward perfection. Perhaps FRŒBEL's successors may further develop his ideas, but another basis than his can scarcely be found, since it is that of nature and truth. He aimed, he says, to find a lawful proceeding, or *method of education*, such as educational science had long aimed to find for *instruction;* and in his system the two are combined—*instruction*, having for its chief end intellectual development, and *education* looking mainly to moral development, or formation of character. The principal requirement for this, is freedom of individual activity, room for the development of individual characteristics. In our present schools all such activity is repressed; children are made to sit still, and on the playground, where the teacher might observe how the children carried out his moral precepts, they are generally left entirely without surveillance or guidance.

But, it is asked, how can there be a law for all? Does not the diversity in creation rest upon the oneness of the Creator? Are not all the heavenly bodies subject to the law of gravitation, and does this hinder individual characteristics? We may accept as certain that each world is different in its organization and productions from every other. So in one forest different plants and trees grow and thrive under the same general conditions of soil, climate, etc., because each individual appropriates of the outward conditions that which is according to its individuality—always the lawful alone. In the universe, it is only *law* guiding motion that makes freedom possible, and prevents destructive conflicts, so in the nursery or kindergarten as well as in the State, only by government according to law can freedom be attained, freedom of each by freedom of all. That education should be according to nature, nearly all, at least, of the modern educators, demand as an essential condition, but according to nature is according to law.

It is lawful and according to nature that the progressive development of single individuals, as well as of humanity, needs in each of its stages new conditions, new means and aids. The glass cover that shielded the germ, can no more cover the full grown tree; a grown up man can wear his little frock no more. The conditions of life, in each epoch of history, in each generation, change, inasmuch as the requirements of each are heightened or raised; therefore the education of our time makes higher and more comprehensive demands of us than were made of the generations before us. Our forefathers, living in forests and clad in bearskins, met the requirements of their time, when they taught the boy to use bow and lance, to guide a horse in the chase and in war, to know the rights and duties traditionally theirs, and the peculiar ritual of their worship; when they instructed the girl in the virtues of her sex, in cooking, spinning, weaving, and nursing the sick. Such demands did not suffice in the later period of chivalry; but even the culture of the knights and their dames, does not satisfy the requirements of our time, because all the conditions of life have changed.

With these conditions, the being of man likewise

changes, in a measure, bodily, spiritually and mentally; not primarily, not in form or shape of his body, not *wholly* in his propensities, inclinations, passions, or in the processes of thinking, feeling and willing. Man has still the same organization, he enjoys and suffers according to impressions received, he thinks and aspires in a human way. But is there no difference between a barbarian and a cultivated man, not only in outward appearance and manifestations, but in inclinations, aims, thought and will? The bodily formation of the working classes is usually modified in this, that their bone and muscle formation is more prominent, while in those of a more intellectual mode of life the nervous organization is predominant. The structure of the head of a thinker differs greatly from that of a savage or a mere mechanical worker. This difference is transmitted to the children; they not only inherit the physical constitution of their forefathers, but very often they also inherit their mental and moral qualities. The child of a Bushman is *born* differently organized from the child of a civilized European, and the child of the nineteenth century is born differently organized from one born in the first century of our time, because the progress of the race will express itself also in the individual.

In plants and animals, we see very clearly the modification produced by culture. The wild carrot, for instance, had to go through twenty generations of cultivation before it became eatable, while, if left to itself, without care or culture for five generations, it relapses into a wild state. The breeder of horses knows very well that the descendant of a noble race is itself noble, and requires greater care and nursing than that of a common breed. And again experience teaches us that it is very difficult to educate the child of coarse, brutal parents for a higher, more cultivated life. The science of mankind has not advanced far enough to be able to show up and fathom the mighty influence of mental culture on our physical and psychical organism; but it cannot be doubted that the higher the culture of a people is, the better endowed its children will be born.

With the recognition of this truth, the necessity for a progressive mode of education must be admitted; and all those who think that what was formerly considered good and sufficient must be good and sufficient now, are mistaken. But each time and generation has certainly some good features, and this in a reform is generally lost sight of. If we must admit that there is a great advance in the modes and appliances for *instruction*, it is equally certain that the preceding generation, so far as *education* is concerned, was ahead of us. Principles of integrity and morals, force of character, and religious fervor, the foundation of a true education, were far more developed among our forefathers than they are now. The physical culture of the ancient Greeks, their training for the development of strength, beauty and dexterity, are not known among us. Then it cannot be denied that a one-sided development of *one* faculty of the mind has prevailed, and a senseless, shallow memorizing of facts, in almost all branches of knowledge, is characteristic of our time. Who can close the eyes on those evils that present themselves so glaringly in our generation, and which are the cause of great misery! A part of the responsibility for these results, education has to take upon itself. We see everywhere knowing without doing, doing without creative power,—thinking, before imagination and sentiment, or feelings, have, as the germ and blossom, prepared the way for this fruit. We see understanding without achievement, the conquering of matter and material forces merely to make them serviceable for the gratification of the senses; we find no veneration for the Spirit of God animating the universe, no faith in Divine Providence, but instead of these man's intellect worshipped and considered his highest tribunal. The feeling of childlike trust and dependence on our Heavenly Father, is dying out, because its source, spontaneity of feeling, is early dried up; the *external*, the most unimportant, is made the most *important;* learning is only taking up what is given, which destroys originality and inherent power. On all sides, we hear a clamor for new rights, without any consideration that there are also duties to perform. And because it is so, a sense of suffering goes through the world, a painful seeking for never-reached happiness agitates mankind, even amidst sensuous pleasures; and, notwithstanding all the gratification that riches and luxury can give, a painful sense of want and emptiness, a longing for something higher and more ideal is, if not consciously felt, still there. We wait for the magic word that shall create a new world, a new generation capable of great deeds, and able to understand the new revelations which God has in store for us.—Who is to speak this word?

Every radical reform, in whatever sphere, needs always a new truth, a new, original idea for its foundation. But such an idea, in its generalization, seldom appears entirely new; the pages of history show that it had been proclaimed, in a different form, by thinkers of other ages, and the same idea always recurring may at different epochs have been striving for embodiment. If this is the case, then we may be sure that it is a very important truth, whose solution, though often attempted, has not yet been realized. Often only one happy hit is needed to make this long propounded problem a reality *. Whether FRŒBEL has

---

* In a Journal of Athens, Greece, "*The Polihistor*", we find: "M. BETANT, Professor of Greek literature in Geneva, has had the kindness to send us some Journals and Pamphlets about Kindergartens lately established. We have examined this method in its principal, leading ideas, and in its particulars, and have found, to our great surprise, the development and realization of what, thousands of years ago, our divine PLATO considered the main point in the development of man from infancy. In adapting education in the kindergartens to nature, and admitting to them those of the most tender age, no other means than play are resorted to.

had such a happy conception in matters of education for giving it a new foundation, experience in the application and carrying out of his system must demonstrate to those who cannot gain this conviction by becoming acquainted with the ideas he embodied in his writings and institutions,—they will have to wait

---

PLATO had the same ideas, as we shall perceive on turning to a paragraph in his "Laws": 'I say that it has been hitherto overlooked in all States that plays have the mightiest influence on the maintenance or non-maintenance of laws, for if those plays are conducted according to laws or rules, and children always pursue their amusements in the same manner and find pleasure in it, it is not to be feared that they will break laws, the end of which is more serious.' In "The Republic" PLATO again expresses himself in much the same manner. He says: ' From the first years, the plays of children ought to be subject to strict laws, for if those plays, and those who take part in them, are arbitrary and lawless, how can children ever become virtuous men, abiding by and obedient to law? If, on the contrary, children are early trained to submit to law in their plays, the love for those laws enters their souls with the music accompanying them, never leaves them, and helps in their development.' In scrutinizing FRŒBEL's method, it is strikingly evident that it is nothing else than a detailed commentary on these words of PLATO, which have hitherto remained unintelligible, unfathomed and unappreciated.

It is easily to be seen that, in our time, when so many new schemes of education have been discussed, FRŒBEL alone has carried out the suggestion that PLATO gave in his beautiful language, and made play the basis of his grand educational scheme, play which he has developed organically in all its directions. The anarchy or arbitrariness of play he subjects to laws; he subjects it even to the laws of rhythm, as PLATO says, because so many of his plays are accompanied by music."

to see the results embodied in those children that have been educated according to his principles.

The most difficult of all difficult things certainly is to give a generally acceptable definition of a new truth, small or great, that lies so much beyond the common apprehension of people. Therefore it was not easy for Frœbel to make himself understood, and his complaint that he was not comprehended was justified, for in his time he was only understood by a few. Still he succeeded in impressing all of his immediate disciples with the importance of his ideas, and the sacred mission devolving upon them; and they have succeeded so far that they have disseminated those ideas in all civilized countries.

Intellectual development likewise proceeds according to distinct laws; these correspond to the laws that govern the universe, being only heightened for the higher grades of development. We must be able to trace this lawfulness to a fundamental law, different as its modes of expression may be on the higher plane. Frœbel calls it, as many thinkers before him did, the law of contrasts and their connection, or the law of equipoise. There exists nothing to which it is not applicable, for everything that exists is a connected contrast. One proposition always presupposes a counter position. God pre-supposes the universe, and the universe presupposes God; man connects nature, or relative unconsciousness, with God, or absolute consciousness. The interior and exterior of an object are contrasts which are connected by the object itself and made *one*. In nature this law also manifests itself as interchange of matter. All organisms have the property of secreting or eliminating substances, and, as a contrast, of assimilating, attracting, sucking up what other organisms have thrown off or eliminated. This is a process of giving and taking, which is by assimilation connected in the mode peculiar to each substance. This is the interchange, by which the material world is in constant reciprocal intercourse which holds it and, as it were, blends it.

In the world of intellect, the same law operates in an analogous manner. Intellectual development is also interchange of matter in a spiritual sense. From without, the soul takes in its store of impressions or perceptions through the senses, to work them interiorly into thoughts and conceptions, in order to manifest them again outwardly as words and actions. Without the society and communion of other men, man would never learn to think or speak. The process of thought is impossible without comparison; in order to compare, there must be differences; the most distinct differences form relative contrasts which find a connection in that which has points of resemblance to each. Thinking, therefore, is a connection of contrasts, or opposites, in the mind. This is also the law of centrifugal and centripetal force, and the processes of inhaling and exhaling, of contraction and expansion, may serve to exemplify the same.

This long recognized law FRŒBEL applied to education, reasoning thus: as this law is active in the process of intellectual development in earliest childhood, in the period of unconsciousness,—that is to say, that as the unaided development of the child must proceed according to this law,—therefore it is the natural, necessary law of the human soul, which education has to take into account, if it aims at proceeding according to nature.

This is done when the educator in his method applies this law, and induces the child also to apply it in his activity or work. This should be done even from the beginning of childish development, from the period of dawning consciousness, which is the starting point of all that is to come afterward. By doing this, the future more or less conscious proceeding of the human mind will be prepared for, while by a contrary or wrong proceeding it will be hampered instead of aided. For instance: the child receives, through the senses, from its very birth, impressions from without; it feels warmth and cold, perceives light and darkness, learns by and by to distinguish hard things and soft, solids and liquids, near objects and distant objects, etc. All these are pointed contrasts. The senses in their undeveloped state are unable to distinguish between a hard object and one a little less hard, between things near and those a very little farther removed. The greater the contrast in the qualities of things,—not the things themselves,—in that which constitutes their difference, the more easily they are distinguished. Distinguishing is the first condition of comprehension. Is it then not proper that we should present to the child the things which occupy its attention, in the form of contrasts, in order to facilitate its perception of them? To make it cognizant of size, we should present to it one object of comparatively large size, and another, the same in kind, of a comparatively small size; in order to make it see difference in colors, we should give it two primary colors in strong contrast, etc. In FRŒBEL's second gift, the sphere, a surface without corners or faces (planes), and the cube, with many faces, corners and edges, are connected in the cylinder which, with its half-round surface of the sphere, and half-plane surface and edges of the cube, is the connection of the two opposites. This gift serves as a good illustration of the law.

By means of these forms, the child receives, through the sense of sight, impressions,—nothing else; but from impressions arise perception and will, and subsequently understanding and thinking; therein lies the importance of first impressions. A child so trained will have clearer perceptions than if left to mere chance development.

As God, the Creator, has in all his creation connected contrasts, or opposites, in order to produce harmony, man also in his works ought to proceed in this way. The musician finds the accord by connecting two contrasting sounds by a third; the painter combines the opposites of light and shade by middle tints; the weaver draws the threads of his cloth in perpendicular and horizontal lines. The child in the kindergarten weaves and twists in the same manner;

it lays one stick perpendicularly, another horizontally, and connects the two by laying a third obliquely. It takes the same stick that was perpendicular, and places it in the position of the horizontal, and so learns that one contrast may be turned into the other, as in planting a tree with the branches downward and the roots upward, the roots become branches and the branches roots. FRŒBEL calls *this* law, "The opposite likes." The child applying this simple law, in thousands of different ways in his plays, is led to *create* or invent; for to create for *man* is nothing else than to produce from that which is given, by means of combination, variety of forms and effects. Without law or method, this is not possible; the proceeding in each work of industry as well as of art, is in its fundamental traits according to law.

If the child has always applied this fundamental law in the development of its own mind, in all its little productions, even in play, without knowing anything further about it than that by its simple application it can produce the most manifold forms, shapes, and figures, still much more has in this wise been done to prepare for future studies than could have been attained by any other mode. To arrange, to classify, to distribute, without which no true instruction, no clear thinking can be, has become the life element and habit. Clearness or distinctness in feeling, willing and thinking or perceiving, is the only true and sure foundation of all culture.

Therefore education should be first required to give

support, according to natural laws, to the development of free activity, to take into consideration the outward given conditions of each epoch of time, of each peculiarity. In short, the perception and application of the universal laws of spiritual development are required,—spiritual being used in the widest sense applicable to intellect as well as to morals and religion.

Nobody will deny that any *practical* invention, however small, to bring education into conformity with the laws of our being and the demands of our time, is of the greatest importance, and must serve to shorten and accelerate the process of remodelling society. A new time needs new and better human beings; to produce them, education cannot do *all* still it can do a great deal.

Chapter V.

The Child's Education.

(Continued.)

Poor Childhood, how many wrongs have been committed against thee! The grown man has weapons of defence in his encounters with suffering, but helpless childhood is exposed to all the blows of wrong treatment or cold neglect. Even tenderness, misapplied, does great harm, and may co-exist with the worst neglect. Many mothers fondly caress their children, who do not administer even to their higher spiritual wants, but turn them over to nurses who may possibly be affectionate and faithful, but who are incompetent to feed the souls of their charges. So the poor defenceless child receives many a wound in the very beginning of life. If childhood were more carefully guarded, how many less despairing and desperate human beings there would be! Much has been said and written about the importance of first impressions, and yet what terrible negligence with regard to them in this germinal period of the human soul! How carefully nature shields her germs, the buds in plants and trees, and how little parents do in this respect!

A young and tender leaf pierced with the finest needle, bears the mark, all through its existence, as a constantly widening and hardening knot in its structure. Many such needle-pricks does the young soul receive in childhood, which in time turn into deformities—bad habits, faults, and vices. Is there a single individual who has not had to bear,—sometimes a heavy burden,—the consequence of neglect in childhood? In infancy each man has the roots of his whole being, and as the root, so the tree. The criminal and the good man, if they could look back through the whole of their lives, would easily trace, the one his bad and the other his good deeds, to the roots resting in early childhood. The cause of moral, as well as of physical diseases, is partly to be found in the inborn disposition, a heritage from parents or ancestors; but it depends greatly upon the first nursing and education whether they will be smothered or developed. *To a certain degree* every faulty disposition can be overcome.

Almost all, especially young fond mothers, think that *their* children, resting so softly imbedded in their love, are not to be pitied, that with every rough air all moral evil is likewise excluded. And yet how much sorrow proceeds from that too great tenderness in mothers, which lacks wisdom and enervates body and soul! But what young mother, in any sphere of society, enters upon the maternal relation fully prepared for her duties and her mission as an educator of her children? Seldom does she possess knowledge so far as healthful conditions for their physical development are concerned. Or if she knows, is she willing to take the exclusive care of her child? and if she employs others, does she always carefully watch that they do not give anything hurtful to the child, or treat it otherwise than they should? Sometimes the seeds of future disease are laid in early childhood. Health is very essential, it gives strength to work and to do good; sickly children are petted and spoiled, and, if they live, are unfit for the various duties of mature life.

But the moral, or rather immoral, impressions received in early childhood, are often more pernicious even than physical injuries. The seeming passivity of the young being often misleads, in regard to its keen susceptibility to impressions from without. It is generally supposed that it is insensible to disorder, uncleanliness, rudeness, and want of beauty in its surroundings, but these first impressions mark the standpoint from which it regards the world. It is said that each of us is the child of his time and of his nationality, and in this is expressed the truth that we reflect the impressions of our immediate and somewhat extended surroundings. In this sense, we may also say, each is the child of his family, his nurse, his nursery, his school, his playmates, for his time and nation are reflected in them. The stamp which body and soul show at a later period, in which the individuality of each consists, is traceable to first impressions that fell like rain or sunshine on the natural, inborn disposition. The boy who is brought up in the tumult of war and camp-life, will have a different impress from one brought up, in peaceful retirement, among the flowers of the garden. The Spartans and the Athenians lived in the same country, under the same climate, at the same epoch, and yet how differently custom and culture colored the characters of the people. Custom and culture proceed from education,—that which is given and that which is taken. That which is principally *given*, is merely the *first* education which fits the human being to *take*, at a later period, that which is needed.

Certainly, few errors breed so much evil, and hinder the development of the good in humanity so much as that of regarding the child, in the first years of its life, merely as a physical being. The great majority of mothers think that at this period the soul is entirely unimpressible and without wants. We have even heard mothers call their children little animals. But if the soul manifests itself later, it must have been in *existence* before, however slumber-like its state, and must have been awakened and strengthened for its manifestations. By what means did it attain such a degree of development? By impressions gradually received from without, by the influence of its surroundings. Body and soul, or the mind and its organs, are, as it were, in the beginning only *one*, and *seemingly* bodily wants express themselves almost exclusively. The organs must gain strength before the soul can use them, but through their development the soul itself grows, and is shaped according to the degree of their development. Every bodily impression—one on the eye for example—is also a soul impression, and the younger the human being is, and the less power of resistance it has, the stronger is this impression. Children adopt readily the manners, habits and moods of their attendants, because in their undevelopment they have no power of resistance, no judgment; they must appropriate external things to their growth, and the external is yet mightier than they are themselves. Therefore they are generally sweet-tempered, good and contented, or cross, sullen and discontented, according to the dispositions of those who surround them. It is wrong to suppose that the coarse, ill manners of servants or nurses, are indifferent to a young child. Anger and lying a child learns nearly always from those around it. To eat things forbidden, to nibble or junket, leads often to theft. Many a promising youth has been lost, because his mother carelessly left things that he coveted lying about, while she had not trained him to resist temptation, or to deny himself any gratification. Later in life, he was unable to endure privations, and gratified his desires at whatever cost.

As in a moral point of view, so in an intellectual one, carelessness and thoughtlessness on the part of parents, in the first years of an infant's life, may do a great deal of harm. Much of the mental confusion, the muddle-headedness of our time, may be traced to the overcrowding of little children, one or two years old, with the variety of toy rubbish that is given them.

How can they ever master it? How can they gain clear, distinct impressions from such things? Inner clearness proceeds from outward order. It would be easier for a grown person to take in, at a glance, all the objects in an industrial exhibition, than for a young child to take in and distinguish between all the different objects that are to serve for the acquisition of its knowledge. It may seem ridiculous to speak of the *knowledge* of an infant one year old; but does it not learn about shape, color, material, size, number, in short, about the qualities of things, before it can reason about them? This it does even in the first year of its life.

It is not expected that a child six or seven years old, with all the necessary materials, books, paper, pen and ink, should learn to read and write without assistance; but it is expected that a child up to its third year should become acquainted, without aid or instruction, in a thorough, practical manner, such as is necessary to form clear conceptions, with all the different objects which surround it, and their various qualities. Without the right materials and without help, it learns imperfectly what it ought to learn well at that early age in preparation for school, be it even for a Kindergarten. Some conscientious mothers occupy themselves a great deal with their children, but not knowing or understanding much about the laws of their mental development, they may fall into grave errors, forcing and stimulating the little brains too much, and thus causing serious injury. This reflection induced FRŒBEL, after he had found and studied those laws of development, to write his book for the instruction of mothers,* and to give lectures to mothers and nurses.

Through the senses, the young soul receives the first nourishment for the development of the mind. As the nature of the first physical nourishment is of the greatest importance in the development of its physical organism, so the nature of the first soul nourishment which the child receives, is of like importance. The development of the soul depends, in a great measure, not only upon the full development of the limbs, senses, and organs, but upon the means by which they are developed. Not more eagerly does the sucking babe take in the milk, than do its senses, especially those of which the eyes and ears are organs, take in food for the soul. In this period, receptivity predominates. As the bee gathers honey from many flowers, so the soul of the child gathers impressions from many images; these must become perceptions before the first signs of intellectual activity show themselves. Up to this period, the soul's powers work interiorly, unseen, like the seed in the ground before the germ appears; but as this germ perishes, if it is not moistened and nursed, so many soul-endowments perish, if they are not supplied with nutriment.

In what then does the first culture of the young

---

* It is hoped that this book, "*Mutter-, Spiel- und Kose-Lieder*" will be translated.

soul consist? Is it not in impressions of the beautiful, the true, the good? These three, beauty, truth, goodness, are the aim of *all* culture, and therefore ought also to be the aim of the culture of infancy and youth. Education must begin with the ideal, and thence proceed to the real, if each generation is to realize new ideas. Imagination should be developed before reason; that it is naturally exercised first, we see in the history of the human race. It is very important that adequate food for childish receptivity—reason being undeveloped—should be found. We have hitherto believed that the feelers of the young soul would find out the necessary nutrition, as the instinct of animals finds their proper food, and therefore children have been left to their own resources. As little as a young animal can appease its hunger in a barren desert, can the child's soul satisfy its hunger, if its surroundings contain nothing on which it can feed. But are not the forms, colors, sounds and materials, which might serve as images for the little child's interior world, everywhere found in nature and the outer world? They are certainly therein contained, but distributed, not collected; not arranged for the eye that has not yet seen, the ear that has not yet heard anything. They are *not* existing in the *elementary* form which the yet untrained senses require. Can the eye of a child, in its first years, see the beauty of a landscape, in its variety of picturesque points, even if it is represented as a painted picture? Or can the ear of a child have an impression of a symphony of Beethoven, even a general impression? It is impossible; for the organs have not yet the power to convey such complicated impressions, nor has the soul the power to comprehend them. Too strong, too powerful impressions, either weaken the young senses, or leave the soul entirely unaffected.

As nature has prepared for the child, in its mother's milk, its fit bodily nourishment, so the mother ought to supply proper soul nourishment. She should collect objects to spread out before the senses, so that the soul in its gropings may find what is fit; and besides this the mother should remove from the child's presence all those things which may be hurtful to its development and growth. She should adapt the large images of nature and the outer world to a smaller compass; she should disintegrate single objects, select them, clothe them with fancy and imagination, animate them, and make them symbols of beauty, truth and goodness, so that they may be apprehended by the simple capacities of the child.

It is not easy to find the symbols for the earliest development; it is an art which requires deep knowledge, knowledge of physiology and psychology;—how are mothers, *all* mothers to gain it? The motherly instinct, the motherly love, are certainly magicians, sometimes making even the simplest perform wonders, and, without the wonders that love has performed, humanity in childhood would have had a still harder struggle to develop itself than has been the case. How marked is the difference between two children of the same age, the one cared for and caressed by a loving mother, the other brought up amid indifference and dull surroundings! How many children, in foundling hospitals, die more for want of soul food than physical care! Still not every mother is able to find all the child's soul needs, if none of its faculties are to remain dormant, if every one of them is to be developed as much as possible.

It is the single individual who finds what *all need*. For all its needs, humanity has had discoverers, inventors, geniuses, who have beautified or remodelled human existence, and supplied the demand for knowledge in various directions. It was FRŒBEL'S mission to make the needs of childhood understood, to fit humanity for a higher step in its development, and to furnish mothers with the symbols by which they can lead the young soul through the labyrinths of its primary stage of existence. His mind selected and arranged the materials, the forms, colors and sounds in elementary simplicity, as they are fitted to enter into the soul life of the child, without disturbing its quiet development as a bud, without awakening the soul rudely or precociously from its slumber, and yet not allowing the glowing spark to be extinguished in the ashes of the materialistic world. He found the true law, by the aid of which the mother's instinct may safely and firmly proceed to find what is needed for the soul nourishment of the young human plant.

What then is needed? Shall we give the young

soul everything ready made, prepared and graded, that it may be saved all exertion, and take it in as it does its mother's milk? Certainly, in the beginning, the child's surroundings should be fitted, ordered and modelled according to its need, even as the cradle and garments are prepared for the babe. The infant has to take everything before it can give; in a few months it reaches out its tiny hands as if to grasp and take its share of the world. FRŒBEL thinks that the first grasping of the child, is the earliest sign of awakening intelligence. It desires to take hold of material objects with its hands, till the mind takes hold too, and grasps in its own peculiar way. Only by appropriation can man come into relation with his world, but appropriation must be accompanied by exertion, since rights entail duties. In the first months of a child's life, self-activity begins, itself a beginning for further exertions; but instead of aiding the child and furthering its efforts, the exercise which conveys an impression of space and distance, is denied it in taking away the object which the little hands reach after and crave to experiment with.

Self-activity is the first principle of FRŒBEL's method. The child, he says, begins its activity by making what is outward interior, that is, it takes from outward things impressions into its soul, in order to manifest, at a later period, the interior as exterior; or, in other words, having converted the impressions received into perceptions and thoughts, it will manifest them outwardly again in its works and actions.

To take in and live out, are as essential to the child's being as to all mankind.

Supposing the child to have been provided with the right surroundings, from which it has taken impressions of the beautiful, the true and the good, how is it to live them out or to show them in its life? How shall self-activity manifest itself? In what form or way shall peculiar individuality be expressed? The child must manifest its inner being according to nature, in the form to which childish instinct leads: *in play*.

Play is free activity, the result of well-being and joy. It is joy and happiness to the child to develop itself in a natural way, though in unconsciousness of the purpose, the aim of its activity. JEAN PAUL says, "Play is the first poetry of the child", but it embodies also its first deeds. After the first months of passive taking in, the child begins the life of acting, producing —sound for example—and later of remodelling; for to remodel the world, is the task of humanity.

The child, one year old, that exerts all its strength to pound an object on the table, to throw it on the floor again and again; that tries to open a door while on its mother's arm, or to pull open a drawer, uses its powers and feels pleasure in the exercise; it plays, but without aim or end in view, and without showing its peculiar characteristics. Grown older, the child imitates in its play. The little girl, for instance, with her doll repeats what is done with herself,—washes, dresses, undresses and puts it to bed. Or children imitate what they see in the kitchen, the workshop, the garden or the street. This faculty of imitation awakens perception in the soul, and leads on to dramatic personification, thus constantly exercising the thinking faculties. At an early age, imitation is mostly of a general character, though differences of sex soon manifest themselves, girls liking different plays from boys; even temperament shows itself early, at least the phlegmatic and sanguine are easily distinguished, and many individual traits mark peculiarity of character. But it is only in rare cases that especially favored, highly gifted geniuses in science and art, manifest their peculiar gifts so early in life. All great musicians have not composed sonatas at six years of age, as Mozart did. Love of nature may indicate the future naturalist, or love of numbers the mathematician. But not in doing and acting alone, will a child manifest its peculiar personality; real productivity or *creative* activity is necessary to bring out individual talents. In the works of its hands we shall find indications of its peculiar vocation. How skilful the little hands of children can be made, we see in the sad spectacle of thousands of young beings, in the manifold branches of industry, used like machines, always in one direction. What a burning shame to our social system, what a blight on humanity, is such a desecration of innocent children!

The mind of a child can only produce inventively, in the joyousness of play filled with the desire to attain a certain result; the wish to gratify its own love for the beautiful, or, from the work of its hands, to make a present to a dear friend, may incite its imagination. For the attainment of such ends, the healthy child shuns no labor, no exertions. Even without a certain end in view, children like to work, to work hard, if it is done like play; it is in their nature, for man was created to work, to be useful. Who has not observed the zest with which children sweep or shovel snow, or do any voluntary work?

But the child must become an artist, within the limits of its powers, if the blossom of its peculiar individuality is to develop. For this, common, imitative, aimless playing does not suffice; for this, it needs guidance, instruction and proper material. How often do the little ones long for, and beg the assistance of grown people in their plays! They feel that they need guidance and counsel. How eagerly do they look round for proper material, by the aid of which they may carry out their ideas! But grown people seldom know how to be true guides; they are either overbearing and arbitrary, desiring children to act according to *their* ideas, or they are without interest and sympathy. They fail to enter into the spirit of the plays, nor do they understand childhood; though every one of them was once a child, it would seem nothing is more easily forgotten! The material which children generally find in their surroundings, is too crude and clumsy for shaping and moulding. For instance, considerable strength and skill are required to whittle wood, and little children can not do it. Ready made playthings leave no room for work, and cease to interest, when their novelty is gone. It has often been remarked, that the childish imagination delights in unshapen things more than in those which are properly finished, to which nothing can be added. Often the child of simple taste, unspoiled by luxury, prefers a bit of wood, or rag, that to its imagination represents a doll, to a real and beautiful one from a shop. Increasing luxury, and the present perfection of toys, serve to make children merely idle observers and critics of their playthings; they soon tire of them, and ennui leads them to the only activity left in regard to them—their destruction. Children become surfeited, want continual change and something new; they are dissatisfied with everything, because in all this abundance there is nothing to give activity to their powers. The building-blocks and tool-boxes now given to boys, are very well, but instruction in the use of them should also be given.

FRŒBEL relates, that when he was a little boy, he became interested in watching the workmen who were repairing the gothic church of the village. After closely observing what they did, he collected stones, pieces of timber and boards, and began also to build a church; but after trying a great while in vain to produce something satisfactory, he gave up in despair. This fruitless attempt, he thought, gave him his first impression that children ought to have better prepared materials to work with, and some one to tell them how to work, and that then they would certainly do better. So his own childish attempts at play, in his father's garden, became the starting point from which he proceeded to find suitable materials and a method of using them,—the occupations and system of the Kindergarten.

These means of occupation serve, even from the first months, to make the perception of things easier. The simplicity, order and adaptation of the objects presented to the child, facilitate its reception of impressions of shape, size, number, color, sound; and by definiteness, succession and connection, distinct images and impressions are given, adapted to the awakening comprehension. They serve to develop the limbs, the senses and all organs, in the pleasantest manner, by *self-exertion*, so that the child is enabled to express what is within, to recognize itself in its own works, even as the work of the artist shows forth his mind. The *childish instinct of play* came to *consciousness* in FRŒBEL; he saw (if we may attribute a sort of consciousness to nature) the end that nature had in view, he saw the analogy between these primitive manifestations in the development of childhood and the development of the human race, or humanity; and thus he was able to find adequate means to gratify the impulse for culture, which is inborn, and by which man develops himself and his world.

It is commonly said that genius always makes its way, that genius will finally triumph. Certainly, Divine Providence finds the means by which those chosen to fulfil a great mission, will attain the end; but who can tell how much sorrow and fruitless struggle, how many tears might have been spared them! or how much greater their accomplishments might have been, how much more genial their hearts, if the struggle had not been so hard! How many of those who finally attain the palm, are soured and embittered in spirit, or broken in health by early privations? Many think that the development of such genius or character is due to these tears, struggles, and despair. It is true that man owes his greatness always to his own exertions, by which he develops natural endowments; but it is of great importance to recognize such endowments in early life, and to take right steps at the outset to attain the ends aimed at. We often see genius break through all obstacles, but we doubt whether such obstacles are needful. If a person who has a beautiful voice never sings, or is never trained in music, how can he become a great singer? If Humboldt and Thorwaldsen had been imprisoned in a dark cellar, where neither sight nor sound could have reached them, where their faculties could not have developed, or even if they had been children of very poor parents, their wonderful genius might never have unfolded. Who may count the fettered powers and gifts that drop from the tree of humanity like unripe fruit, because they had no scope for exercise, because the soul was never brought out from its darkness! It is not probable that the number of geniuses will diminish, if their crown of thorns is changed to a crown of roses, when all their powers find scope for joyous working and striving, and wise guidance makes clearer to the child even its true calling, and shows it the shortest way to attain it. All the overexertions of humanity should be done away with, especially in childhood, for children ought above all things to be happy. They become happy by activity, by developing their dormant powers. Their real wants should be gratified; they should have exercise, and by it instruct themselves, without the deadening constraint of the school.

The awakening of the *creative* spirit in children, will free the coming generation from its greediness for pleasure and excitement, which unsettles the morals of our own generation. Activity as play furnishes the elements of all knowledge, and the capacity *for doing*, so that a connection and unity in culture are brought about. Knowing and doing are separated in our day, theory is apart from practice, which is an evil in morals as well as in science. The school ought to receive the child already prepared with the fundamental conditions for the acquisition of knowledge: the child should be able to see with its eyes, to hear with its ears, to observe; it should be in a receptive state, having a desire for knowledge, able to distinguish the objects in its surroundings, and able to give expression to its inner world, in forms that are in accordance with its childish ways. The clay modelling in the Kindergarten is, of course, very imperfect, compared with the modelling of the sculptor, but it is the child's mode of expressing its simple ideas and conceptions.

Virtue and morality must be taught by practice, words and precepts are not sufficient; by exercise only the will gains strength for good and noble actions. There is no better field for children to learn to practise virtue in than is given in the Kindergarten. The restraint is not too great, and the children are among their equals in age, toward whom they will freely act out themselves, as they would not do toward older people.

No epoch requires *doing*, so much as the present. The achievements of industry in our day, are as colossal as the pyramids of Egypt; but instead of requiring centuries for their accomplishment they require only days, and the external world is remodelled with great rapidity. But how slow is the progress of moral reform compared with this! What power can we employ to rival in its effects the wonders accomplished? Is there a higher power than love? God's love created the world; and what earthly love is mightier than that of the mother? The divine spark of love is purest and strongest, I might even say holiest, in the mother's heart. Ought it not then to be powerful in purifying and elevating human society, in helping it to rise out of the ashes of bygone centuries to a new life?

It is not sufficient that saving ideas are announced to the world; devotion, patience and sacrifice are required to carry them out practically. Humanity has, as it were, two elements, the masculine and the feminine; hitherto the masculine has predominated, and given its stamp and impress to the world. Dry intellectual culture, and matters of fact, have desolated the world and made it barren, only the dew drops of affection can fructify it again. The appeal that summons women to the rescue, that calls out their activity, is heard everywhere. A cry of distress comes from helpless innocent childhood; it appeals to the heart of the mother to help to form a new and better generation fit to inhabit and give moral strength to the outwardly beautified world. A key has been found to decipher and develop the child's whole being, the alphabet of which is the book for mothers. Will they avail themselves of it, and will young girls gladly consecrate themselves to the guidance of childhood, the sacred office to which FRŒBEL calls them?

Chapter VI.
Frœbel's Mother Cosseting Songs.

This "Family Book", as he calls it, FRŒBEL offers to mothers as a guide for the first infantile development, by means of physical play exercises. The examples given are intended to make clear to the mother's consciousness the aim of all her play with her child. No dry, pedantic imitation is desired, but it is hoped that mothers will imbibe the spirit of the book, and carry out, with such modification as may be necessary, its pervading idea.

For centuries, the mother's instinct, impelled by the desire to amuse her child, has been inventing little plays for the exercise of its limbs, which have, of course, contributed somewhat to their development, but only in an imperfect way, as everything must be that is left to instinct alone. This playing is often nothing but foolish dandling, because mothers or nurses have not the proper end in view,—the development of the limbs, and the wakening of all the dormant faculties of the soul.

A great man has said: "Let me make the songs of

a nation, and I care not who shall make the laws." Perhaps he did not overestimate the influence of song on the hearts of men. How we love our national songs! In proportion as they are the embodiment of justice, truth and purity, in that degree will they be powerful in awakening like sentiments in the hearts of the people. What then should be the character of the songs given to the little child, as the first means of bringing it into conscious relationship with the world around it? Should they not be of the best, the purest type, and at the same time of greatest simplicity? Should not everything that would give the child bad impressions be excluded?

The cradle-songs which have been handed down from one generation to another, through nurses and mothers, are nearly alike in all civilized countries, because they have originated in a maternal instinct which is everywhere pretty much the same. Of such traditional lore FRŒBEL collected what would serve his purpose, while, for the greater part of his life, he carefully observed the simple habits of mothers among the people, entering peasants' huts, and staying for hours with mothers and their babies. He also collected the quaint old sing-songs and lullabies, but freed them from rude, coarse expressions, and from images ill adapted to childish conception, which made those old melodies extremely nonsensical and often hurtful.

No mother plays with her child silently; every one speaks or sings while she plays, because human beings need language from the very beginning of their existence, as a distinctive characteristic of their spiritual nature. Those who yet recollect, with tender emotion, the lullabies with which a mother's voice hushed them to sleep, will understand FRŒBEL who sees in the songs, which accompany the first infantile plays, the means of developing the child's emotional nature. Through musical sounds the heart speaks, and harmonies awaken emotions. But the mother is too often ignorant of the great power that she may wield in this simple element of song; she sings because her heart prompts her to sing; but FRŒBEL sees in her simple song the greatest educator of the infant's soul. He has given to the mother a volume which cannot be too highly valued, the aim of which is nothing less than the development of the child's threefold nature. By the exercises which accompany the songs, physical development is assisted; by the words which always have reference to something nearly related to the child, he is brought into loving sympathy and close relationship with nature and surrounding life, thus developing mind and heart. The mother should always feel that it is her privilege and duty to help the little one to get possession of its powers of body and soul. Soon it must live, think, and feel for itself. The great question for the mother should be: How can I best prepare my child for this independent life of thought and action, how lead it into the right channels? The mother is to the child the world's interpreter. All to the young being is new, strange and wonderful; and is it not well that it does not at once particularize?

Otherwise it would be bewildered by the infinite variety presented to it. It is the mother's mission to enter into the child's nature, to live its life, to understand its impulses, to feel its needs; to bring her love, her sympathy, her wisdom, to this work of leading the child along the dark path of early life, and to make it acquainted with its relations to nature, to its fellows, and, through these to bring it into a conscious relationship to its Heavenly Father.

In the first years of life, physical development is foremost, though the development of the soul proceeds at the same time, for soul and body are so united that the one can only be developed by means of the other. So, according to FRŒBEL's idea, the mind receives the necessary aid to its awakening, through the development of the senses and limbs.

Gymnastic exercises for larger children and for youth, are now almost universally regarded as necessary, as conducive to physical health. But the moral power of man also needs discipline; with the strengthening of the muscles the will-power also strengthens, and with grace of body refinement of soul should likewise be gained. If the young limbs need this varied and systematic exercise for the muscles, after the child can walk, run and jump, how much more do they need it before self-activity begins? Acrobats and circus-riders take only quite young children to train for their callings. The practice of tying up babies in swaddling-clothes has long been abandoned; but when the babe lies with unfettered limbs on its mattress, when it moves hands and feet and plays with them, it needs more aid than an older child, in order to attain the development which these instinctive motions indicate and aim at.

Common gymnastics are designed to exercise and develop every muscle. But such exertion alone would tire the young child too much. Its interest must be awakened in various directions, that it may be happy and joyous. A child will not grow weary of showing its height, while it would be unwilling to stand erect or to stretch out its arms to no purpose. There must be a meaning in all that is done with a child, suited to its comprehension, such as is furnished in FRŒBEL'S play gymnastics. The exercise of the body is in them made also an exercise of all the soul organs, as it were, and the first playful activity of the child becomes the germinal point and the preparation for future development in the kindergarten and school, establishing system and connection throughout the whole process of development.

FRŒBEL himself says of his book: "I have embodied in it the most important ideas of my educational system. It is the starting point for an education according to nature's laws; it shows how all the germs of human endowment have to be nurtured and assisted to produce a full and healthy development." Our poet SCHILLER had a glimpse of this when he said in "Wallenstein": "Deep meaning often lies in childish play."

The modes of expression in "*The Mother Cosseting Songs*" have been criticized as uncouth and often unintelligible, but the critics have not penetrated deeply into the contents or the spirit of the book. They may perhaps improve the form, but let them beware of altering the character of childlike naïveté and originality, in which the charm of the book consists, and which gives it its value. We must not forget, in judging it, that the mottoes are meant for grown people, and the songs for children.

Life is exertion of power, and all adequate exertion is joy in existence. The young animal in its playful capers shows this, as well as the child in its expressions of gladness when it presses its little feet against an object which resists the pressure, or against the hands of the mother, who should repeat this exercise and several of a similar kind, in order to strengthen the muscles of the back and legs. The most important exercises in FRŒBEL'S book are for the hand, as the most important tool of man. The more man is relieved from hand drudgery in work, by the use of machinery, the more the skill of the hand must be developed, that it may be employed in the constantly advancing works of industry and art. The hands of little children among the poorer classes are mostly stiff and clumsy, still they must serve to gain daily bread. Without early exercise, the elasticity of the hand is lost to a great degree, the muscles do not gain sufficient strength to meet the demands in the higher technics of our day. Complaint of the want of skilled labor is universal. Sculptors and great players on the piano or violin know that, only by constant practice in early childhood, could they have overcome the technical difficulties of their arts. The necessity for making use of early childhood, in order to be prepared to meet the demand for men who *know* and can *do*, is, on the whole, more and more felt. Education therefore must begin with overcoming matter, in order to produce change in matter,—in industry and art; and further still to spiritualize matter, so that it may become embodied thought, as in a creation of art. It not only saves time, but a large amount of tedious drill at a later period, if a certain degree of mechanical skill is acquired by means of play in childhood. It is gained almost unconsciously then, and FRŒBEL'S systematic plays not only aim at this physical training, but at the development of mind and soul, thus preventing idleness, the worst enemy to morality and childish innocence. If the mind and the hand work together from the outset, there is little chance of the human being becoming a mere mechanical drudge.

In his book, "*The Mother Cosseting Songs*", FRŒBEL takes into account, as he does in all his other devices for the education and development of children, the threefold relation into which every human being enters at birth, namely the relation to nature, to man and to God. The surroundings of the child are either products of nature or of human culture, and have their final cause in God. The child's relation to these objects should be taught in a manner clear and definite, though connected.

When the little one is taken out into the open air, it will first notice objects in motion, a flag flapping, or a weathercock turning it may be, and when the child is old enough to understand the words used, such a hand gymnastic as FRŒBEL gives, may be employed to illustrate the effect of the wind which, we say, also moves the trees, the mill, the kite. Let the child, too, seek the wind: it cannot be found, and thus the impression of something that acts while hidden—of an unseen force—will be made on the tender mind.

The Weathercock.
Exercise for bringing the Muscles of the Hand and Arm into Action. *

---

* It may be thought strange that instead of a woman's delicate hand a masculine hand is represented in the woodcuts, but they are taken from the original, the model for which was FRŒBEL's hand. Although FRŒBEL had no children of his own, his peculiar faculty of playing with babies was remarkable, and in his lectures to mothers and nurses he always illustrated the play gymnastics of his *Mother Cosseting Songs* himself.

Motto for the Mother.

If you wish your child to find
A lesson suited to its mind,
In all its eyes can see;
When the things you show and name,
Teach it to imitate the same:
The child will learn with glee.

Song for the Child.

Like the cock upon the tower,
Turning round in wind and shower,
Little children's hands must learn,
All in play, to twist and turn.

Sympathy with all created things should be early awakened. The child should live much in the open air, in the country if possible. It realizes no distance, and the little song about the moon shows how FRŒBEL would bring the young soul into loving relations with all that exists in nature.

The Child and the Moon.

Motto for the Mother.

Why do the objects far away,
To the child's eye, so close appear?
Why does it ever wish and strive
To bring the things of distance near?

Mother! canst thou not see in this
A meaning deep, a mystic sign,

Stamped on the babe's unsullied soul,
In wisdom, by a hand divine?

It tells thee not to break the dream
The blessed dream of infancy,—
In which the soul unites with all
In earth or heaven, in sea or sky.

It tells thee that the bounds of space
Exist not for the infant's soul.
All that the senses can perceive,
Seems one great and continuous whole.

And lies there not a truth sublime
In these perceptions of the babe;
A symbol of the highest law,
That the Most High to creatures gave?

A symbol of the law of love!
Oh, mother! let that plead to thee
To teach thy child in God to find
The source of love and unity.

Then break not suddenly the dream,
The blessed dream of infancy;
But teach the opening soul in all
An everlasting love to see.

Come child, come, let us look up at the moon
Now shining so brightly on high;
" And will you not come down to us, bright moon,
From your beautiful home in the sky?"

"Oh yes," says the moon, "I should like to come,
And visit a good little child;
But I cannot get out of my dark blue home,
So I send down my beams so mild.

"'Tis a very long way 'twixt you and me,
Though so near I appear to your sight;
I am much farther off than I seem to be,
But not too far to send down my light.

"And though I can never come down to play
With the good little children I love,
I can often come round, at the close of day,
To shine on them all from above.

"Then very good friends we can ever remain,
Though we live so far off from each other;
Be a very good child, and I'll soon come again
To shine upon you and your mother."

Song for the Child.

"Yes, friends we must always be, beautiful moon!
And whenever you shine from above,
We shall greet you with pleasure; so come again soon,
And with love I shall pay back your love."

The cultivation of the senses is very important, and a very different matter from the gratification of the senses. True, high and noble enjoyment can only be had through their discipline and culture, the sole means of averting low, coarse sensuality so unworthy of man. The sense of taste is the first to develop. The child should not be allowed to devour its food greedily, but be made to distinguish different kinds, as, in a higher sense, the taste is afterwards to be developed and cultivated. While she feeds it, the mother should sing to the child a song indicating the sources of some articles of its food, or allow it to feed animals while it eats, giving a share to the cat, the dog, or the bird. In this way the child's attention is diverted, and directed to something higher than mere self-gratification, though care must be taken that the child, easily interested in other things, does not neglect its own food. FRŒBEL gives the "Mowing Song" for use in the early training of the sense of taste.

Mowing.
Exercise for the Muscles of the Arm and Shoulder.

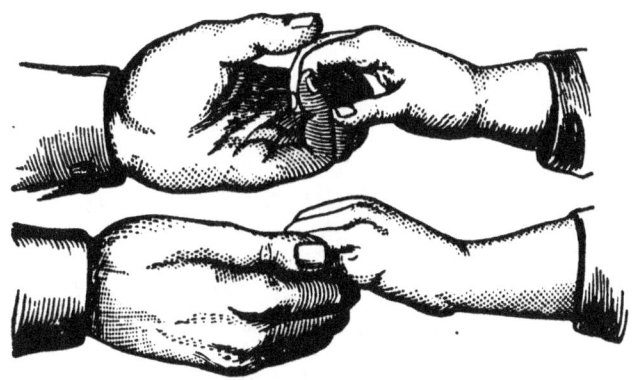

The action of mowing is imitated by the mother taking the child's hands in hers, and swinging them to and fro.

Motto for the Mother.

When the infant's laugh so clear
Rings upon the mother's ear,
And she swings its arms in play,
Let her swing them not in vain;
But let the merry infant gain,
By something she can do or say.

Song for the Child.

"Peter! quick! go out and mow,
In the pretty green meadow;
Then give the grass, so fresh and sweet,
To the gentle cow to eat.
Mary! go and milk the cow,
And make the butter for me now;
From the milk is made the butter
Which I get on bread for supper.
Happy little child am I;
I must never, never cry.

"Peter, quick! go out and mow,
In the pretty green meadow;
And when, this evening, for my supper
I sit and eat my bread and butter,
I must thank you, Peter, for the grass,
And thank the cow, and thank the lass
Who milks the cow, and makes the butter,
And for the bread must thank the baker,
And thank mamma for all, nor let
My heart a single thank forget."

The play of "Pat-a-cake" is almost everywhere played with little children.

The sense of smell should also be cultivated, by causing the child to smell different flowers. A little song, illustrative of this, is made into a play in the Kindergarten.

Love for animals should be early cultivated. Frœbel would have a bird in a cage hung near the child to awaken its interest. Children naturally notice and watch animals. The song of the "Barnyard Gate" in Frœbel's book, is intended to make the child acquainted with the various domestic animals, to teach it their names, and lead it to imitate their voices.

The Bird's Nest.

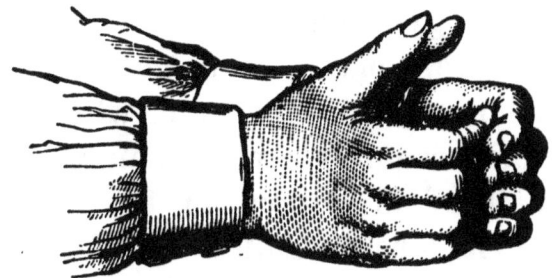

The hands form the nest, the thumbs turned inward represent two eggs. At the words "Soon wee birdies", the thumbs rise and flutter.

> In the hedge a birdie dear
> Builds a nest of straw and hair,
> Lays two eggs so small and round,
> Soon wee birdies there are found.

> They call on mother: "hear, hear, hear,
> Mother so dear, mother so dear,
> Oh mother dear, hear, hear, hear!"

"The Bird's Nest" is made the means of showing the relations to father and mother, and it may also be used to convey to the child first ideas of the protecting care of the Heavenly Father. "I have based my education on religion and it must lead to religion," said FRŒBEL. As we make the young child understand that young birds wait patiently in the nest for the return of the mother who brings them their food, we teach that in like manner it must learn to trust in its Heavenly Father.

"The Watering Pot", another play, which the child has as a hand gymnastic, will lead it afterward to take pleasure in tending and cultivating its little garden patch in the Kindergarten, where it will learn that everything requires care and nursing; that love must show itself in action, in the performance of duties; that it must manifest itself in overcoming laziness, and must shun no trouble. If the child thus early takes loving care of plants and animals, it will afterward be more ready to sacrifice ease and comfort for the sake of dear friends; and so the tendency to selfishness will be early counteracted.

The child's intimate relation to its mother does not cease with its birth, but takes a new phase. Without a mother's love, without a mother's care, entrance into life becomes a sad thing; through her the child is introduced into this world, and she is the interpreter of the world and of humanity, making the young being acquainted with father, brothers, sisters, and friends. With the power to walk, the entire dependence of the child on the mother gradually ceases—only *gradually*, for the physical oneness lasts, as it were, even beyond the period of birth. But, in this first stage of life, there must be established a soul-oneness, if, as the physical union and dependence diminish, the spiritual bond, which gives to the mother the greatest educational influence, is to increase. How touching to see the little child, in its first attempts to walk alone, rush back to its mother's arms, as if in dread of separation! If the hearts of the mother and child are united, during their physical oneness and the period of nursing, then the child's physical independence brings about the reverse in the spiritual relation. The consciousness of its mental dependence on the mother grows in the child, together with the consciousness of bodily independence and the growth of its personality.

According to FRŒBEL, the first manifestation of the relations of love which bind the child to the mother, is its smile. Man alone can smile, and the babe has only this language for the expression of its joy. All relations begin at one point, with one object, and must concentrate there before they can expand. So the mother must become the child's centre around which it moves, till others can approach it; therefore no other person should be so much occupied with the infant, in order that it may thus learn to concentrate itself. The children of the wealthy, who go from arm to arm, and often see little of the mother, are apt to become fickle and less affectionate.

PESTALOZZI in his book for Mothers, as well as FRŒBEL, indicates that when the mother first begins to occupy herself with her child, she should play with its limbs, and this she does, rightly enough, instinctively. By touching the various parts of its body, and naming them to the child, it first becomes acquainted with its own form. The first and the last knowledge that man acquires, is of himself.

He must know himself bodily before he can know himself mentally. The study of physiology is too much neglected in schools. It is a natural instinct that leads children to try to learn about their own forms, by playing with their limbs, and the mother's instinct aids them; but it makes a great difference whether she does it from mere instinct, or intelligently, keeping in view, as an end, physical development.

In the family, the mother must lead the child to understand its relations to the father, the relatives, and the inmates of the house. In the first months of its life, the child recognizes no one but its mother. It is only later, and when it has become acquainted with the members of its family, that strangers or little companions should approach it. We often see babies cry or look frightened when taken among strangers. We say they are shy, and certainly anything unknown, strange, without connecting link, frightens a child. If we wish it to develop harmoniously and lovingly, the little heart must not be crowded, and the circle of relations must not be extended too far at an early period. It is wrong in strangers and grown persons to kiss and caress a young child against its will; violence is done to it, and its life element is taken away.

For all these reasons, it is an injury to the child, if instead of knowing family relations it is immediately introduced into a large community where no tie is so closely woven. The best public institutions, Orphan Asylums, and the like, cannot wholly replace the family, the atmosphere of life in which God has placed the human plant; but in the nurseries and infant schools established according to FRŒBEL's principles, the best is done to give to the poor motherless children motherly care and sympathy, not only in the supply of physical needs, but in satisfying their craving for love, and gratifying their instinct for play.

Father, mother, and child are necessary, says FRŒBEL, to constitute a *whole* human being. The family is the first link in the organism of mankind, the first community. If this first link is imperfectly developed, how can the succeeding ones, he asks, develop perfectly? Still, if this circle, which is the basis of morality, did not enlarge, these exclusive family affections would become family egotism, of which the world is full enough. In the isolation and seclusion of the middle ages, this family egotism was, in a measure, a necessity, and so far was justifiable. Might prevailed over right, and men were separated by family feuds and banded together in clans. In the present century our condition and necessities are different. We are equal before the law, and family egotism, as it exists yet in aristocracy of birth or wealth, in the spirit of exclusiveness, must be rooted out, if love for humanity is to grow.

Therefore the young child, after it has become perfectly familiar with the members of its own family, should enter into a larger community, especially into one where it will find those of its own age. There is instinctive sympathy among children in the same stage of development, as in later periods of life those who are animated by like feelings and thoughts, or have the same pursuits, are attracted toward each other. In fine weather the Kindergarten is the best gathering place for young children, even before the second year. It is far better than public promenades, streets and squares, though the little ones must, of course, always be attended by their mothers or nurses, while they observe the amusements and occupations of the older children.

The family relations are also shown to the child, by means of hand plays given in "The Mother Cosseting Songs." A branch with many buds will suggest to an older child these relations. In the two largest buds it will see papa and mamma, in others brothers and sisters according to size. The little girl plays father, mother and child with her dolls, as well as her companions. These examples show that the family relations are the most natural ones, and those which mostly occupy children. In early childhood, everything must be seen in symbols which give clearer ideas of the objects than the objects themselves. In one of the finger plays, the father, mother and children—including the little one itself—are represented, counted, and named. Again, while the mother presses the fingers one after another, she says: "For the thumb I say one, for the first finger, two, for the middle finger I say three, for the ring finger, four, for the little finger, five; now we have put them all to sleep; they sleep soundly and sweetly. Be quiet that none may awaken too early!"

Counting is an almost inexhaustible pleasure for little children, as everything is which serves for their development, if it is only given in a way they can understand. It is easy to make them aware of number in the measure of music, the rhythm of poetry, and in various other movements. The little game with the fingers serves also for the very young child as an exercise in self-control. Nothing is more difficult for it than to remain perfectly quiet without motion, without sound. You may command silence, without any apparent necessity for it, in vain. But here it comprehends the meaning of the play, and we have seen little children, with a very important air, keep perfectly quiet, holding the hand still many minutes, with the idea that they must not wake the sleeping children. Of little ones only little things can be demanded. Only in such playful ways the child gets conceptions, and a little exertion gradually increased, makes finally the greatest exertion possible. Laziness in children often results from the care which parents take to save them from all exertion, to have everything done for them.

In another play, the fingers are made into a flower basket, in which the child carries flowers to its father. Thus even the youngest finds means to practically show affection for its father or other friends.

Flower Basket.

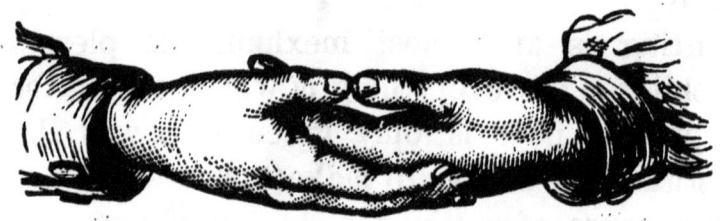

MOTTO FOR THE MOTHER.

What the pretty babe requires,
To call its feelings into play,
The mother's tenderness inspires;
The infant owns the parent's sway.

SONG FOR THE CHILD.

Little hands can learn to make
A basket in a minute,
And mamma can quickly take
Some pretty flowers to fill it.
The basket is not broad or long,

But flowers look cheerful there;
We'll give them, with a little song,
To papa, when he comes here.
Sweet flowers, you are for papa;
La, la, la, la; la, la, la, la.

FRŒBEL says: "Human life must appear to the child as a whole, indicating to it its individual destiny." The child must learn to feel itself a link in the great chain of humanity, and to forget self in doing loving acts for others. It is an essential, leading idea with FRŒBEL, appearing in his book as everywhere else, that the connection among things, as well as among men, should be made plain to the child's mind.

There is a tendency in this age to form associations for the accomplishment of certain ends. If family associations could be brought about, for the purpose of improving educational science and harmonizing its different methods, they would be of greater benefit to the race than all the combinations for material and industrial purposes alone. For such union the Kindergarten affords the best opportunity. It begins education in a community of families related by friendship, where every member has a chance to use his talents for the benefit of the young generation.

Chapter VII.
Froebel's Mother Cosseting Songs.
Continued.

There are in the life of adults, as well as in the life of nations and humanity at large, epochs which exercise a formative influence on it. Something similar takes place in the life of children, and FRŒBEL points out to mothers that by taking advantage of certain moments the right educational influence is derived. The less the child's consciousness is developed, the stronger will be the moral effect of those incidents that seem to us trivial. If the importance of such events were rightly estimated; if the impression made by them were not too quickly effaced, and so the true effect disturbed, the whole moral development would rest on a firmer basis. Everything, even the smallest incident in the life of the infant, is of importance, because it is the beginning of all that is to follow. For instance, FRŒBEL considers the child's first fall as one of the most important events in its early development, the effect of which should not be disturbed. The child's courage in running, proceeds from ignorance of danger; it is like virtue which has been neither tried nor tempted. The child falls, and its security of ignorance is at once shaken. Friends who rush to the rescue, lamenting over and petting it, are unwise. Even though it should be a little hurt and scream in consequence, it should be left to itself long enough to receive a full impression from this first fright and hurt. Then caution awakes, self-confidence is no more blind, and the necessity for gaining strength and skill is learned by degrees. Nothing renders men more superficial than a quick succession of impressions, of which the one effaces the other without leaving any distinct trace in the soul. The present generation, especially in "high life", furnish proof of this. Fast reading, fast travelling, the crowding of all kinds of enjoyments, even the higher ones of nature and art; the pressure and hurry of life, more than anything else, make great numbers in our day superficial, empty and wholly devoid of the spirit of poesy.

As we can trace all the culture of man back to its starting point in the influences of nature, so we shall find that the awakening of conscience proceeds in a manner analogous to the processes of nature. As clearly as we recognize natural laws, do we see that neglect of or want of conformity to them, is outwardly and visibly expressed in physical disease and suffering. In the moral world, the violation of moral law is expressed inwardly by the voice of conscience, and its outward manifestation we call sin.

The importance of the first plays of children has not yet been sufficiently recognized. They are a manifestation of the character of the human being in its first appearing, and as such worthy of study, not so much in their form as in the indications which they furnish. Here again those who do not understand the soul of the child, who have forgotten their own childhood, may smile, because we see in those simple plays the germ of the soul-life, the seeds of spiritual development. But if the first plays of the child, its first childish utterances, are not in connection with the last works of mature age, there is no coherence in human life, no consecutiveness in the development of man's spiritual nature. Only when this connection is fully understood, and education does not sever the thread which unites the child with the youth, will manhood and old age realize their ideals. Then true men, noble characters, will be developed. Humanity must again be brought into close contact with nature. Natural sciences should be more studied with nature herself as the text-book. But that this may be done, we must begin to give to babes the symbolisms of nature, which they understand better than anything else. As humanity in the early dawn of its life understood the language of nature, and heard God's voice in it, so the child understands nature's language of beauty and poetry; and to give it artificial things instead of natural objects, is a cruel wrong. FROEBEL says in relation to man's unity with nature: "What God has united man shall not sever."

A well-known play, pleasing to the youngest children, is "Hide and seek". The face of the older person, or of the child, is covered with a handkerchief, and when this is withdrawn the child will manifest lively pleasure. FROEBEL says of this play: "That which everywhere, among the smallest children, causes a manifestation of joy, a play everywhere played with them, must have a deep significance,—of that you may be sure." Let us see how he interprets it for us. The joy which the child manifests on seeing the mother again after separation, proceeds from the deepened impression of union with her given by means of the contrast. But if the concealment last too long, or if the mother fail to show her joy at seeing the child again, it may cause disappointment, and awaken a liking for concealment in the child, which may lead to lying, or the concealment of the truth. Who can tell how the first germs of evil in children come, and how they are indicated? The least spark which illuminates the darkness of the first psychological processes in the human soul, is of importance, and FRŒBEL has certainly looked deep into the original soul-life of the child. Good and bad are closely connected, and as God's Providence often turns bad into good, so education should seek to turn the tendency to evil into a channel for good. At the point where the danger of leading the child to secretiveness comes, help should also come. If the mother make this an occasion for deepening in the child's mind the impression of its unity with her, everything is gained. Outer separation gives the sense of inner connection, for everywhere unity is the end, and separation merely the means to bring it to perception. This is FRŒBEL'S explanation of the play, and it agrees with his law of contrasts and their connections, which he applies on the moral plane as well as in his occupations. He never leaves a discord or contrast till it is resolved into an accord or unity by connection.

The most essential thing in the child's education, is the establishment of full confidence in the mother (as well as later in the teacher), so that it may not attempt to *hide*, in case it should commit a fault. But this confidence can only be secured by living with the child its own life, by playing with it, by entering sympathetically into all things which move its soul, and in rightly understanding and rightly guiding the manifestations of its first development. Has the first fault been committed? *Loving* sympathy with the first interior suffering of the child, as with an evil he has himself brought about, is often more effectual than the severest blame. That this blame must, sooner or later, be expressed, is certain, but it is always better to make the child see the real consequences as the effect of the fault committed. A look, a gesture, be it of gladness or of sorrow, the smallest child will understand. The moment of the first wrongdoing is therefore very important, because it is the point at which conscience awakens. That it may listen to this inner voice, it is essential that a child should learn to listen to an outer voice, to a call, to pay attention to it, if it is addressed to itself. FRŒBEL links this to the play "Cuckoo, Cuckoo", in which the child, not seeing the mother, hears her voice and rejoices over it. If a child is taught to listen to and obey its mother's voice leading to what is good and right, it will learn to listen to its own inner voice, nor leave it unheeded. If a mother has secured the child's joyful obedience to her voice, because she has never commanded what was contrary to its highest good, and has studied not to require what would be subversive of the child's personality, then she will easily teach it to love and to obey the voice of conscience, or God's voice, that will accompany it through life as a guardian angel; and she will make it see that this is a relation connecting man with God. The same relation which exists between the child and the mother, when it begins to distinguish *its* will, its *personality* from hers, will afterward be recognized by the child, as existing between its individual inclinations and the warning voice or judgment of conscience. If there are love, loving obedience and perfect trust between mother and child, instead of fear of punishment and severity, then true morality and dignity, which do not act from inner or outer constraint, will guide the child; it will love the good for good's sake; it will obey the inner voice from free choice, from love of God. Man may become a morally free agent, or he may be a slave to his own passions, or do the behests of others, from flattery, threats or promises of gain held out, and for each condition the foundations may be laid at this early period of life. The character of a man does not depend upon the number of his failures, but upon the manner in which he rises and makes amends for the faults committed. In our time and in this country where obedience to the authority of a *person* is not demanded, it is evidently of the greatest importance that education should aim at developing obedience to *law*. Parents must early show the child, that they too, that teachers and all grown persons, have to obey a superior; that they can not do as they please in violation of the right any more than children can. This should be done to awaken the idea of lawfulness and morality, an idea which becomes the governing power, when children have *outgrown* the *authority* of the parents.

All the good and rightful qualities of the child, may be reversed and become faults. Early education has, generally, to deal first with wilfulness or obstinacy. Without self-will character could not be developed. To insist on one's own peculiarities, one's own opinion, one's own will, till overruled by something higher, is right, because upon this is based self-responsibility or that which constitutes man an accountable, free-willed being. The child's obstinacy is the reverse of this awakened personality. Obstinacy may be aroused by doing something that the child dislikes, or refusing it something that it wants. If what it desires is legitimate, something that serves for its sustenance or development, then the child is in the right; but if it is simply unwilling to submit to a reasonable demand of its elders, it is wrong and must not be listened to. If a babe screams in its cradle for want of nourishment, or because it requires attention, it should not be left unheeded a moment. If it is neglected, the tone of its cry changes into that of obstinacy and anger, and the attendants are to blame; but if it screams merely because it is more agreeable to it to be taken up, it should not always be gratified, lest it become wilful and tyrannical toward attendants. Certainly it is reasonable that a child should want what is agreeable, and dislike to be left alone and unoccupied; but it must early learn to submit to conditions; to miss sometimes, for a season, what is most agreeable, and submit to what is less pleasant, for the sake of others. This, however, must not be carried too far or last too long, and necessary attention ought never to be withheld. It is difficult to do always the right thing, but love, the highest principle, allied with wisdom, is the safest guide. The child should obey from love which awakens energy for good, not from fear which makes cowardly. From loving obedience springs veneration which leads to the fear of God.

In education, wrong obedience is often mistaken for right obedience, that is, the child's will is broken instead of turned into the right course; and it is for this reason that so few persons are self-centred, or inwardly free and able to govern themselves. FRŒBEL'S general rules are to leave the child as much as possible to itself, without commanding or forbidding, and to allow it to gain its own experiences so far as that may be done without injury. It would not be difficult to secure the child's obedience, if the right means were adopted. Children, as well as animals, have instinctive perception of good intentions; a look into the eyes suffices to cause a feeling of trust or distrust toward those who have them in charge. The main point is to awaken love, and gain the child's confidence, never asking anything beyond its strength or capacity. In the beginning, it is better to avoid, as much as possible, requiring what is distasteful, only by degrees demanding what involves self-denial, what is difficult or unpleasant. The foundation of obedience, as well as that of all other virtues, is laid in *early* childhood. Some of these virtues are, in the main, only good habits acquired then, and afterward not difficult to retain. FRŒBEL has given excellent advice and hints to mothers in "*The Cosseting Songs*", and therefore they are invaluable aids in moral training.

In its relations to men, after a knowledge of those most intimately related to it is gained, the child will be led to observe the life of the various trades and professions. It must become acquainted with the functions of human industry, with *work* in its manifold forms. The little child likes to imitate in play the motions made in planing, sawing, threshing, boring, etc. This imitation will lead to more careful observation of those occupations; the different motions employed will impart flexibility to the hand, and, by developing its skill thus early, prepare the child for its own future work in life. Such daily gymnastics may be made the basis for a first fulfilment of duties, and will fit the child to perform them. A play called "The Carpenter", serves to awaken love for house and home. Children love to build houses, if it is only with chairs in the corner of a room, but while love of home is cultivated, exclusiveness and family egotism should be guarded against.

The Carpenter.

The house is represented by the position of the fingers; the two thumbs moved as if hammering, represent two carpenters working on the crossbeam. A little song accompanies this play as well as all other plays.

In "The Charcoal Man's Hut", the child is taught the dignity of labor, and that useful work, even though not clean, is honorable. Let it be told how many useful things are made by means of charcoal: knives, forks, spoons, nails, etc., and that although the charcoal-man's hands and face are black, his heart may be good and true.

"The Market-Booth" is designed to give an idea of commerce, but the ideal side should be represented; and the child should understand that a great deal of labor is required to make all these nice things. It should be made to see that this exchange is one of love, and be led to anticipate with pleasure the time when, grown a man, it may contribute its share of useful labor to the community. If children are taken to fairs, it is not well *always* to buy presents for them. They should learn to see and admire things without greedily wishing to possess them.

One powerful means of awakening the ideal side of the human being, is the early cultivation of art; and the blending of art with industry in our time makes it almost a necessity for all grades and classes of society. There is hardly any branch of industry in which drawing is not required. Music is more and more cultivated by all. "The Finger Piano" is an exercise for the fingers, and accompanied by song cultivates the ear, teaches time, rhythm and lawfulness of motion. Rattles, bunches of keys, all discordant noises, ought to be given up; songs, some pleasant instrument, the sounds of nature, are best for the young child. One of the greatest singers of our age, Jenny Lind, says, that her musical talent first showed itself and began to develop at the age of four years, when she went into the garden or field, and tried to imitate the songs of various birds and the hum of the bee or fly.

According to FRŒBEL, drawing is to be one of the first occupations of the child, because in this employment it can most easily produce something. It likes to follow the contours of objects with its fingers, and in this way gets a more accurate idea of the forms. To facilitate the child's instinctive manifestations in this direction, FRŒBEL would have the mother spread sand on a table, and let the little one draw figures of familiar objects upon it, e. g. a window with lengthwise and crosswise marks. In giving the child other than objects themselves, we should choose the image of the thing rather than its sign in letters and written words; therefore linear drawing ought to precede writing. We see in Egyptian art, which may be likened to the drawing of children, only outlines of things,—no perspective.

But even before a child can hold a pencil, it can lay little sticks—embodied lines—in various forms, for, from the beginning, FRŒBEL would have self-activity, creative self-activity, cultivated in the child. He often repeats: "Let us try to have the child embody all its perceptions in actions, only thus can laziness and inertia be overcome, even from the beginning". It has not been known hitherto that even the smallest child ought to be led to *do* something to satisfy its natural craving for activity, which if disregarded will be turned into inertia. The laying of sticks, or drawing, serves to teach a child much about shape, size and number. It should not be merely receptive, and thus collect an incongruous mass of forms and images which are never used. What it has received interiorly it should express outwardly; this is what the child wishes to do, but the means are often wanting. Observe children standing at a window. How eagerly they watch men and animals passing in the street, or notice the opposite houses! If they happen to have a slate and pencil, they often try to reproduce what they have seen with a few lines; and very lively children will imitate the motions of passing objects. They love to play horse, they get on hands and feet to run like dogs, etc. The wish to imitate is the first *incitement* to activity, but it should not rest there, it should lead to free activity, to invention. Though it have slate and pencil, the very young child can not reproduce as it would like; it can not yet hold the pencil, it can not yet draw, it is soon tired of the few marks which it makes at random, because they do not represent what it wishes; and soon it falls into a habit of vacant staring at things without distinguishing them.

How very little scope and aid are given to youthful activity! Yet if it is not fostered, it is deadened; idleness becomes a habit which the children at last come to like, while they dread every exertion. It would seem that nothing is thought of but to make the child receive first with eyes and ears, then with the mind, learning and learning but never *doing!* FRŒBEL teaches, on the contrary, that the child should not see, hear or learn anything which it can not, by reproducing, make its individual property; and, as we have seen, he furnishes the means for accomplishing this, in early drawing,—the earliest in sand, in stick laying, easier than drawing, and in the modelling in clay, thus preparing the child for artistic productions.

In his book, "*The Education of Mankind*", FRŒBEL says: "The faculty of drawing is as natural to the child as the faculty of speech, for word and sign are as closely related as soul and body". When in all the departments of the child's *knowing*, the application of it, the *doing*, is intimately connected, and every peculiarity finds its means of expression; when the works of little children make them conscious of their own creative power, and disclose their talents and inclinations, then the children of a future day will not, as is now the case, be crammed with dead knowledge, and presume to judge of everything in a critical, precocious manner, without ever *producing* anything, unable to act with force and power. In what are called the higher classes of society, the young people now-a-days know a great deal too much or, at least, think they know very much. They can not condescend to *do* anything, and prefer to produce nothing. In the lower classes again, young people are mere drudges or machines, and thought is unconnected with their work. The true balance between receptivity and productivity has been lost and must be re-established. This may be done by FRŒBEL's method; by it early childhood is instructed through that which it produces and experiences; *doing* is from the start made the *source* and the companion of *knowing*. In a moral point of view too the child is first made to act according to moral law, before it is taught morality in the form of abstraction or precept. True morality is only evinced in action.

As we have found that the human being, following a general law of nature, develops according to its species, and have seen that it bears a threefold relation,—to nature, to man, and to God,—we must now look into FRŒBEL's ideas concerning the development of the religious side of the child's nature, or its relation to God.

The belief in a divine Being, in God, is inborn; it is an intuition, a germ contained in the soul, that may be developed or neglected. As every spiritual development, all consciousness, proceeds from undefined perceptions and feelings, so the perception of God, or Deity. But as no development proceeds without outward stimulation, without means adapted to the end, so childhood must have, as humanity had, a revelation, bringing the unconscious groping and longing into consciousness, giving expression to feeling and a definite shape to faith. But how does God manifest Himself to the young child? Is this possible in the first year of life? We may say that the childish unconsciousness is a resting in God, a union with God. That which is not separated from us is not objective, for we cannot place ourselves in contrast with that which is inseparable from us. While the young child is unconscious of self-existence, is not yet a conscious personality, it is one with everything that surrounds it, and is in close relation to it. Therefore FRŒBEL says: "The child is in *unity* with nature, with man and with God". It lives yet in Paradise, in the time before the disruption,—previous to the inner and outer separation,—as mankind did in the beginning. It can have no religion, for that implies a striving after unity with God, and no one strives after what he already possesses; only when something is lost which is seen to be a good, does man strive after it. The word, religion, expresses the idea of reunion with God: "God-union" FRŒBEL calls it. When the child first fails in good, the unconscious union ceases and discord steps in.

In the visible world the child is in closest union with its mother. The disposition, the tone of mind, or the passing feeling of the mother, is immediately transmitted to the child. If she is frightened, the child is also frightened without knowing why. FRŒBEL considers it a difficult problem to know when and how to influence the child, and nurse the divine spark within it. He says: it is like the seed germs in spring, which exist long before they are visible to us; or like the stars which, astronomers tell us, have their places in the heavens long before their rays reach our vision. But the time when this religious development in the child begins we can not mark exactly. If we begin our nursing too early, it may happen, as with the grain of seed which is exposed too soon to the rays of the sun, or receives too much fructifying moisture—the tender germ will be blighted. But if we come too late, or our efforts are too feeble, we may likewise fail. What then is the part of education according to FRŒBEL? He would have the beginning made cautiously by means of impressions only. A child one or two years of age is magnetically impressed, if it sees its parents engaged in pious devotion. One can not *talk* to so young a child about God.

Music enters the human heart, and awakening indefinite longings impresses the soul, therefore FRŒBEL desired the mother to sing sometimes sacred music to the child, or to play simple melodies upon a melodeon or an organ.

Next to sound, gesture impresses a young child. The folding of the hands, on going to bed, indicates that they have now nothing more to do, and suggests concentration, inner collection, as the plant folds up its leaves at night. At first the mother will pray for the child, and when it can understand, it should join in the words, but not mechanically; the mother should direct its thoughts to all the good it has received during the day, awaken gratitude toward all those who have contributed to its happiness, and finally to the Giver of all good. In such a frame of mind, the simple words: "Dear God, I thank Thee", are a true prayer. If a child has done wrong in the day, how easy to bring the fault to its remembrance, saying that not only its parents but God was grieved, and then lead it to ask His forgiveness, and help to become better! The early teaching of dogmas, Bible history and Bible verses, which it can not comprehend, tends more to weaken and deaden all religious feeling than to awaken it. Only what the child experiences within itself, is full of life. The mind and heart must be *prepared* for religious teaching; more can not be done at this age.

The history of creation as recorded in Genesis, if told to the child, is far less comprehensible, than the idea of God, the Creator, which comes into its mind, when it is shown examples in nature, and led to observe their life and growth. For the gaining of such knowledge, a garden, in which the child may plant seeds, is of inestimable value. Things which engage its activity make lasting impressions, and it soon perceives that of itself it can make nothing grow.

That christianity should become active is the need of our time. FRŒBEL says: "Faith comes through love, but love cannot exist without manifesting itself. You can not do heroic deeds in words or by talking of them. You can educate a child to self-activity and to works, and through them to a faith which will not be dead." In the "*Mother Cosseting Songs*", FRŒBEL wished to give to the child the elements of all culture; and the idea of religion is conveyed in the hand gymnastic called "The Church Window." The fingers are intertwined to represent a gothic arch, and with the accompanying music give the impression of community in worship, etc. Religion requires the giving up of one's self to something higher, the surrender of our own personality and self-will. But we must love the Being to whom we thus give ourselves. Before the child can love God who is invisible, it must love visible men. It first loves God in man, in its parents. All primitive religions required sacrifices, such offerings signifying the giving up of egotism, of personality, without which a consecration to God is not possible. If the child is always accustomed to manifest its love in deeds, when grown up it will not merely talk about Christian love and charity, but really exercise those spiritual graces.

If the child has gained a general idea of God, the Creator, in nature, it must also in man learn of Him as a Person. As humanity needed the manifestation of God in the flesh, as an ideal after which to strive, so childhood needs the ideal found in the Child Christ, a picture of whom, represented either on His mother's knees, or in the Temple, should be hung up in every nursery and every kindergarten. All the good qualities of children may be ascribed to Jesus, and they may be reminded that Christ was always obedient, grateful and loving. In thus connecting the child's inner and outer life with the childhood of Jesus, a complete ideal is furnished, and by linking with it the events of His further life on earth, Christmas as His Birthday, etc., historical knowledge may be given, but mere dogmas should not be taught at this age. Anything of which the child can form no conception, confuses its mind and hinders development. It is not wise to take young children to church constantly, before they can understand anything of public worship or preaching. Sunday schools are well if conducted in a manner adapted to childish needs. A child can not become religious without means and help, any more than it can without them become intellectually wise, but it is essential that the right means be used, the right help given. We should see to it that the coming generation imbibes the *true* spirit of the Christian religion, so that it may show it forth in a new phase of humanity.

Chapter VIII.
Fundamental Forms.

How do we arrive at diversity of colors? By mixing or combining. If we analyze combinations of colors, we receive the three primary ones, red, blue and yellow. All study of colors, every employment of them, must start from this basis. A painter really needs only these three; all others he can produce by combination. A child needs, in addition to these, only the first mixture; the others it will be able to make for itself, if the rules are given. Explain to it that by mixing red and blue we have purple; that blue and yellow make green, yellow and red, orange, and it will go on making combinations according to the law. How is variety of melodies produced? By combinations of sounds. Analyzing these combinations, we arrive at the simple elements of sound. Musical knowledge must begin with these elementary sounds and their names. The combinations follow laws similar to those of color. How is the variety of human features brought about, so that no two men look precisely alike? It is by combinations of the hard and soft parts of the human countenance which vary in size and form. Of the number of varieties thus arising we gain an idea, if we suppose merely thirty differences in each bone composing the face to be possible. For instance, if we allow to the forehead ten different heights, breadths and curves, we shall have about 1,000,000,000,000,000. The letters of the alphabet and their innumerable combinations into words in different languages, furnish another example of this law.

Now let us ask, how does the untold variety of *all* natural objects, and of all the productions of human hands, originate? Are there any fundamental forms, original models, by the different combinations of which every form that exists has been produced? If so, can we by analysis of such combinations arrive at these elementary forms? Must we have a knowledge of these, in order to understand natural objects, and in order to produce any kind of form ourselves, even as, in beginning the study of music and painting, we must acquire a knowledge of elementary sounds and colors? Certainly, it cannot be otherwise. The law is universal. What then are these original models for the creative, formative imagination and hand of man? They are the fundamental, geometrical forms of planes and the solids proceeding from them. By analysis of these planes in their diversity, we get the point, the line, the angle,—right, acute and blunt,—the triangle,—right, acute, and blunt angled triangles,—the four cornered forms,—the square, rectangle and parallelogram, and so on; according to the number of sides and angles we find the pentagon, hexagon, octagon etc., till we reach the many-sided form, the polygon, and, finally, the circle comprising within itself all corners. Adding the oval, or ellipse, we have all the fundamental forms of the planes,—elements of form analogous to the elementary sounds of music.

By variation and combination, the diversities of planes and solids are produced, and these can be easily reduced to their fundamental forms. From the triangle result the prism, the pyramid; from the square, the cube; from the rectangle, the parallelopipedon; from the polygon, the polyhedron; from the oval, the lens. These are the fundamental forms of the solids, the original models for the creative human brain and hand. He who would understand natural forms, or the creations of art, must start with a knowledge of these primary figures. Their existence was demonstrated by Pythagoras, two thousand years before Christ, but their importance in organic and inorganic nature was not recognized and duly estimated before our own time. Linnæus pointed to crystal forms as a key to the recognition and classification of minerals. Rocks and stones and everything they include, are crystals agglomerated into masses, each crystal having one or another of these fundamental forms. What wonderful harmony and simplicity of idea these structures embody! It would seem that the all-wise Creator of the world has shown us by example, that a great variety of elements is not necessary to a great result! But these fundamental forms are likewise the basis in organic nature, and by their various combinations all corporeal things exist. The human mind can only reproduce, and the human hand can only imitate what is given in nature. Man therefore works according to and with these fundamental forms. All drawing deals with points, lines, angles, triangles, squares, many-cornered forms and curves. The numberless combinations of these make images which again are but imitations of nature or natural objects. Every branch of industry, of trade or mechanics, uses as a basis these primary plane forms, working from them according to the models of the corresponding solids. Art and trade must build on these forms, as the musician must base his harmonies on the elementary sounds. If man should disregard these simple forms and laws, deeming them unimportant, if he should refuse to study them and their combinations, then the material world would be closed to us, for without these there is nothing to be learned or worth the learning. Yet how little is really known about such forms and laws by those who should know most!

The mason cannot do without his plummet, or the carpenter without his square, but how many know the meaning, the importance of these necessary tools? How often we hear mechanics say: "That is all useless theoretical trash! you have to learn your trade practically." Owing to this want of knowledge, work is too often done mechanically and stupidly. Man should no longer pass unheedingly by natural laws and forms, and all these necessary things ought to be taught in schools.

No subject of knowledge is so near, so essential to man, as a knowledge of nature and her laws. But geometry, the basis of all natural science, should not be taught at the outset as an *abstract science*; it is not likely thus to awaken interest in many youthful minds. But if it starts from the original, fundamental forms of nature, and never loses its connection with them; if its single tenets and laws are deduced in organic connection clear to the pupil's consciousness, then no thoughtful person, no one who is interested in the contemplation of nature, will pass this fundamental science by with indifference. How great would be the benefit to industry and the life of the nation, from such a popular and universal knowledge of geometry and the natural sciences resting upon it, if we could succeed in teaching the coming generation, from earliest childhood, to think over again the grand creation of the universe, to reproduce it, as it were, in their thoughts! FRŒBEL conceived the importance of such an effort, and therefore *he made the eternal archetypes of nature the playthings of childhood, and the laws, mutual relations and combinations, which nature employs in her secret workshop, the child's laws and rules of play.*

We see then that the great variety of natural forms surrounding us results from the combination, according to certain laws, of a comparatively few elementary ones. We see further that before we can rightly understand the compounds, we must know something about the simple elements of which they are composed. Now when a human being awakens from its dreamlife, it is confronted with this great variety, and instantly begins its efforts to make acquaintance with the world that surrounds it. Its attempts appear to us in the form of play. The child knows nothing, and ought to know nothing, of the seriousness, the hardships of work; but if we leave it entirely unaided in its efforts, do we make its task easier? Some say, it is best to leave the child entirely to itself, to race and tear, romp and play as it pleases, but is it not in a sense unkind and barbarous not to reach out to it a helping hand, as it seeks in its childish way through much difficulty to gain experimental knowledge of things? We should guard against too great or prolonged exertion of the young body or mind, keeping from the latter abstract ideas, while we seek by every means to convey correct impressions, and so raise the whole development, placing it upon a more perfect plane. These clear impressions may be received in play, and they will aid the child gradually to attain a true knowledge of objects, in its immediate surroundings and in nature.

The first occupation with external things, should begin with the elementary forms and models that we have considered. The simplest of these is the sphere, and it best conveys the idea of unity. Without corners, edges or sides, it demands no distinguishing faculty in the child. The simplest of all differences, those of color, are alone presented in it. Hence, to the infant awaking from its slumber, FRŒBEL gives in succession six worsted balls wrought in the three primary and three secondary colors. The form of the sphere is the most perfect in nature. As the circle may be considered the perfection of planes, including them all, so the sphere is the perfection of solids, in which all others are comprehended. The heavenly bodies are all spheres, our earth is a sphere, producing an infinite variety of forms. With the largest sphere the inorganic world ends, with the minutest, the microscopical cell, the organic world begins. The human organism also begins existence as a cell, and thence arise all the organs. From the sphere the whole organic world proceeds. Look then at the importance of the ball as the first plaything of the child! It is the simplest of all forms, and therefore best adapted to give first impressions to the tender mind; yet by suggestion it encloses the whole universe even as in the child may be seen the future man.

The idea of the relation of the ball to other objects, is not to be given at this early stage, for the child can perceive only one thing at a time. But this one thing is here, there, up and down in space, disappears and comes back at intervals in time. First impressions, I do not say perceptions, of space and time so difficult for a child to master, are thus given with its earliest toy. Such are the principal ideas underlying the first gift.

The second gift consists of a wooden sphere, cylinder and cube. Let us look at the significance of each of these objects. The cube is second to the sphere in simplicity of form. Having corners, edges and faces answering to points, lines and squares, it presents greater variety than the sphere, but, like it, shows one and the same form on whichsoever face it may rest. The ball is alike on all sides; the cube shows differences but not in a bewildering degree, only in a way suited to develop the child's faculty of comparison. The cylinder is the connecting link between the two. The plane of the sphere is the circle; this is seen in the circular faces of the cylinder, and the likeness to the sphere is also traced in the cylinder's round sides. We have before noticed that the circle includes all forms, therefore in it we have the square which from its simplicity has been adopted as a normal standard of measurement,—the square inch, foot, etc. From the sphere proceeds the form next in simplicity, the cube, likewise a normal measure,—cubic inch, foot, etc. If we suspend the cube and turn it in different ways, the double cone, the wheel, and the cylinder appear,—the three fundamental forms of mechanics, and their future importance is thus foreshadowed. After giving these impressions, the three objects are used in play; and as impressions with regard to time and space were conveyed by means of the first gift, in this the child gains an idea of sound connected with motion in a hard body; of rest becoming motion as this body is moved. The cube rests and must be pushed, it will not roll. The child must see that where the cube is, the ball cannot be, that each object occupies space. In the change of form caused by rotation, he will also distinguish between what is permanent and what is transitory.

The third gift is a cube divided into eight smaller cubes. This division gives for the first time the impression of measure. Out of the *oneness* of the cube results *manifoldness*, though the many are like the one in form, and equal among themselves. Hence impressions of resemblance, similarity and difference in their finer distinctions, are made. The practical use of number is also in this gift extended. From the whole come the halves, quarters and eighths. Each little cube is a part of the large whole. By means of this cube, the child is now able to embody or express what is in its mind. In its third year, it is so far advanced, that it notices differences in number, shape, and position,—it begins to think. It can also gratify its desire for activity, in making forms of life, or use, forms of beauty, or symmetry, and forms of perception, or knowledge, by the division into halves, quarters, etc., with regard to different directions in space. The forms of perception address themselves to the mind and understanding; the forms of beauty cultivate sentiment and feeling; the forms of life lead to a close observance of objects, and to a knowledge of their practical uses in human society.

We need only say further that FRŒBEL's Gifts pass in orderly sequence from the divided solid to the surface, or plane, which is first presented in the square, and afterwards in the various triangular forms, through a series of tablets. Next the embodied line is given in small staffs of different lengths, and at last the point is indicated by the child in its employment of pricking. Thus passing from the concrete to the verge of the abstract, correct impressions are constantly deepened, and the way prepared for true perceptions. Nature furnishes the models and the laws for the natural development of mind.

As this is not a Kindergarten Manual, we do not enter into all Kindergarten occupations in detail, and even the best guide that could be written would not suffice for the instruction of kindergarten teachers. We wish merely to show, by a glance at the manner in which geometry is made the foundation of knowledge, that what is considered only play by a superficial observer, has a deep, scientific basis which the *teacher* must *perfectly* understand, though the *child* is not yet *conscious* of it. The two extreme objections raised by persons unaware of the true import of kindergarten culture, the one that it is mere play, and the other that little children are over stimulated by it, and taught a science so difficult as geometry, thus correct each other.

Chapter IX.
Reading.

It may seem superfluous to speak of the time-honored custom of teaching the child, first of all, to read, since in the foregoing pages we have shown that such a custom is contrary to the natural order of development. But prejudices are generally firmly rooted, and unless we clearly state Frœbel's reasons for not wishing to begin the child's education with reading, its exclusion may be considered a mere whim, and its introduction into the kindergarten exercises a harmless practice.

We have found that orderly development leads from the real object to the image, and from the image to the symbol or sign; and if we look back in history and see how long mankind lived and progressed before book knowledge formed any prominent part of life or education; if we consider the complicated forms that compose the alphabet, it will appear reasonable to argue that the child's eye should first become familiar with simple forms; that its perceptive faculties should be somewhat developed, so that it may be able to compare and distinguish, before the alphabet, in itself wholly uninteresting, is presented to it.

But people say: "Children like to learn their letters

at a very early age." If they do, is it not because parents stimulate, praise and reward them for their efforts to master them? The hungry child will take almost any kind of food that is offered to satisfy its bodily hunger, even the unpalatable if very hungry; and it is only natural that it should take whatever mental nourishment is offered, however unsuitable, if it is starving for want of that which is adapted to its faculties—the case nearly always in the early years of life.

I can not help a deep feeling of pity for such hapless children, when a mother tells me with pride that her child four years old already knows his letters! Poor little creatures! all their hard striving to obtain knowledge of the various objects that surround them, the many useful things that they truly and honestly learn without help, often in spite of hinderance, in the first years of their lives,—all go for nothing! They are called stupid and dull, if they fail to master those cabalistic signs! Parents are so impatient to have them little grown-up men and women. To be a child and do childish things is considered almost a disgrace, something to be ashamed of, or like a disease to be got rid of as soon as possible. But is the life of grown-up people, into which parents are so anxious to initiate their children, a thing so delightful, so much to be desired, that they should barter all the innocent joys and delights of childhood for it? We think not.

But, it is urged, there is so much to be learned in

our day, no time should be lost, children must begin very early, else they will not be able to learn all that they ought to know. Is intellectual culture then all that is necessary, or the most important? Granting, even, that it is, do we lose time, if we postpone reading and writing to the age of seven, as FRŒBEL proposes, and, instead, send the child from its third year to the kindergarten where books find no place? Experience teaches that when children so prepared enter the primary school, they soon distance others who have for years sat listless, through weary hours, to the detriment of health, over the printed page.

Does not American history show us that its so-called self-made men, who have generally learned to read later in life, have been more than others distinguished for executive ability, originality of thought and practical energy? And here we touch upon another of FRŒBEL'S reasons for wishing to keep books away from young children: he desired to save them from habits of mental indolence induced by feeding upon others' thoughts, without the necessity for self-exertion. In their state of mental receptivity, he saw the danger of overfeeding, of stifling productivity; he wished to make even the very young child a creative agent.

When the child has reached its seventh year, we would strongly recommend the use of Dr. LEIGH'S phonic method in teaching it reading, which has been introduced with the best results into the public schools of St. LOUIS, and into some of the schools in BOSTON and NEW YORK. We have ourselves tested its practical value in an advanced class, and know that children with previous kindergarten training learn to read in an incredibly short time, requiring only a few minutes of instruction each day. This phonic method, or pronouncing orthography, has, in our opinion, many advantages over former ones, but we cannot here mention all. It serves our present purpose to state that we deem Dr. LEIGH's method entirely in harmony with FRŒBEL's system. It gives for every sound a sign, and children can intelligently compose or build up their own words, or dissect and separate them again into their constituent parts, as they have been used to do with their building-blocks. Their self-activity is thus incited to acquire the knowledge of reading in a far more interesting and rational way than in mere memorizing under the old methods.

Let us not be understood to advocate letting the child run wild till it is seven years old, on the contrary we deem it important that it should be acquiring habits of concentration and application, not by means of abstractions, but through interesting employments, such as the kindergarten furnishes. The advantages of kindergarten training over the ordinary primary school system are so many, and can be so easily deduced from what has already been said, that we need not attempt to enumerate them. It will readily be seen, that there is no art, science or industry, which, in its first principles, is not represented in the occupations of the kindergarten.

The children are not merely theoretically prepared for whatever may be their future pursuits in life; but practical *doing* goes hand in hand with theory. It is evident, that this method can and ought to be carried beyond the age of seven; that theory and practice should not be separated in our higher schools; that older pupils should have the advantages of Industrial, Scientific and Art schools (the Boston Institute of Technology is doing an excellent work in one direction), which would enable them to perfect themselves in any special calling for which the kindergarten develops an aptitude and lays a foundation.

HORACE MANN'S estimate of the spelling-book is seen in the following quotation: "In Scotland the spelling book is called the 'spell book', and we ought to adopt that appellation here, for, as it is often used with us, it does cast a spell over the faculties of children, which generally they do not break for years, and oftentimes, we believe, never. If any two things on earth should be put together and kept together, one would suppose that it should be the idea of a thing and the name of a thing. The spelling-book, however, is a most artful and elaborate contrivance, by which words are separated from their meanings, so that the words can be transferred into the mind of the pupil without permitting any glimmer of their meaning to accompany them. A spelling-book is a collection of things without the things signified—of words without sense—a dictionary without definitions. It is a place where words are shut up and impounded, so that their signification can not get at them. Yet formerly it was the almost universal practice—and we fear it is now nearly so—to keep children two or three years in the spelling-book, where the mind's eye is averted from the objects, qualities and relations of things, and fastened upon a few marks, of themselves wholly uninteresting."

The spelling-book is not yet obsolete, and though we are aware that it has been improved by the addition of definitions for the more difficult words, still the definitions are often as unintelligible to the child as the original words.

Publisher's Advertisements.

E. Steiger,

22 and 24 Frankfort Street, New York,

keeps on hand an

Extensive and well assorted Supply of

Kindergarten Gifts (Occupation Material),

of foreign as well as domestic manufacture.

Particular attention is called to E. STEIGER'S Stock of

Books and Pamphlets

—in German, English and French—

ON THE

Kindergarten System.

The New Education, as FRŒBEL'S System is properly called, is here represented in all that is requisite to its integrity and full development, by every publication of note on the subject issued in

America, Germany, England, France and Belgium.

E. STEIGER'S Agents in Germany, England, and elsewhere in Europe, are instructed to forward new publications appertaining to the Kindergarten System immediately on their appearance.

The following pages contain

a Portion of E. STEIGER'S Stock of Kindergarten Literature.

All publications are in paper covers, unless otherwise indicated, as: cart. (cartonnirt) = in boards; geb. (gebunden) = bound; Lwd. (Leinwand) = in cloth; Goldschn. (Goldschnitt) = gilt edges.

Some other Abbreviations:

Abbild. (Abbildung) = figure; Abth. (Abtheilung) = division; Bd. (Band) = volume; Bdchn. (Bändchen) = part; Dr., dr. (Druck) = impression; e. (ein, etc.) = a, one; erkl. (erklärend) = explanatory; Fig. (Figuren) = figures; Hft. (Heft) = number, part; hrsg. (herausgegeben) = edited; Hlzschn. (Holzschnitt) = woodcut; illum., illustr. (illuminirt, illustrirt) = illuminated, illustrated; m. (mit) = with; Tab., Taf. (Tabelle, Tafel) = table, etc.; Th. (Theil) = part; u. (und) = and, etc. etc.

Kindergarten und Kleinkinder-Unterricht.

F. Altmüller. Blüthen aus dem Garten der Kindheit. Ueber die Entwickelung der Seele des Kindes. Mit 1 Titelbild in Holzschn. Herabg. Pr. cart. 1.05

F. W. Andreä. Die Kleinkinder-Bewahranstalt, nach ihrer Nothwendigkeit u. Einrichtung, ihrem Aufwand u. Segen, insbesondere auf dem Lande. Mit eingedr. Holzschn. 0.20

E. Bircher. Jugend-, Turn- u. Gesellschaftsspiele für Kindergärten, Turnanstalten u. Gesellschaften. cart. 0.45

v. Bissing-Beerberg. Was noth thut, oder die Kleinkinderschule u. was zur Förderung derselben zu thun. Mit 1 Holzschntaf. 0.45

J. F. Bofinger. Die Kleinkinderschule u. Kinderpflege Württemberg's. 0.50

A. L. Charles. Die Kleinkinder-Bewahranstalt. Ein Büchlein fur Schule u. Haus. Mit 8 Holzschn. 0.45

H. Deinhardt u. Chr. Gläsel. Das Stäbchenlegen u. die Erbsenarbeiten im Volksschulunterricht. Als e. Grundlage des Zeichnens, des Rechnens u. der geometrischen Formenlehre. Mit 40 lith. Taf. 1.00

F. A. W. Diesterweg. Der Unterricht in der Klein-Kinderschule oder die Anfänge der Unterweisung u. Bildung in der Volksschule. 0.65

C. Döring. 62 Spiele für Knaben u. Mädchen zum Gebrauche bei Schul- u. Kinderfesten, Spaziergängen u. anderen festlichen Gelegenheiten. 0.25

G. Engelbach. Beziehungen der christlichen Kleinkinderschule zur Kirche. 0.25

Die erste Erziehung durch die Mutter nach FR. FRÖBEL's Grundsätzen. Mit Holzschn. u. 4 Taf. 0.45

I. H. v. Fichte. Die nächsten Aufgaben für die Nationalerziehung der Gegenwart m. Bezug auf FR. FRÖBEL's Erziehungssystem. Eine kritisch-pädagogische Studie. 0.35

A. S. Fischer. Anregung zur Errichtung e. Bildungscursus für Gehülfinnen an Bewahranstalten, Bonnen u. Kindermädchen. 0.20

J. Fölsing. Erziehungsstoffe in Gedichten, Märchen, Gesängen, statistischen Nachrichten, erziehlichen Rathschlägen u. Winken aus dem Gebiete der Kinderstube u. Kleinkinderschule zu e. naturgemässen Entwickelung der Kindheit. Für Väter u. Mütter, Erzieher u. Erzieherinnen. 3 Thle. 2.30

—— Zur Reform der Kleinkinderschule. Beiblätter zu den Erziehungsstoffen. 0.50

J. Fölsing. Die Menschenerziehung, oder die naturgemässe Erziehung u. Entwickelung d. Kindheit in den ersten Lebensjahren Ein Buch für das Familien u. Kleinkinderschulleben. Herabg. Pr. 0.45

—— Geist der Kleinkindererziehung, insbesondere die Kleinkinderschule, wie sie ist u. sein soll. 0.45

—— Ueber Kleinkinder - Schulen, Wohnstuben u. Ausbildung deutscher Erzieherinnen. Skizzen aus dem Leben, als Beitrag zum Fundament bei e. Neubau deutscher Erziehung u. Gesittung. 0.25

—— Die hessischen Kleinkinderschulen nach authentischen Quellen zum ersten Mal zusammengestellt. 0.20

—— Anklagen der Mängel in den Bewahranstalten für Kinder vor der Schule u. Mittel zur möglichsten Beseitigung der Missstände. 0.15

—— Die Kleinkinderschule zu Darmstadt m. Beziehungen auf ähnliche Anstalten in Deutschland. Vortrag. 0.15

—— Geschichten für Kinder. Müttern, Geschwistern, Erziehern u. Erzieherinnen dargebracht. cart. 0.65

—— u. C. F. Lauckhard. Pädagogische Bilder, oder die moderne Erziehung der Familie u. Kleinkinderschule in der Nähe u. Ferne betrachtet. 0.65

—— —— Die Kleinkinderschulen, was sie sind u. was sie sein sollen. Zum Fundament beim neuen Aufbau des Volksschulwesens. 0.65

A. Frankenberg. Der Kindergarten als Berufschule für Jungfrauen. Ein Plan zur Bildung junger Mädchen nach dem 14. Jahre. Mit 1 Tab. 0.20

A. Frantz. Blicke u. Winke in die Kinderstube. Treuen Müttern wohlmeinend dargeboten. 0.45

Frdr. Fröbel. Gesammelte pädagogische Schriften. Hrsg. v. WICH. LANGE. 2 Bde. in 3 Abthlgn. 10.00

I. Bd. 1. Abthg.: Aus FRÖBEL's Leben u. erstem Streben. Autobiographie u. kleinere Schriften. Mit FR.'s lith. Portr. 2.95

I. Bd. 2. Abth.: Ideen FR. FRÖBEL's über die Menschenerziehung u. Aufsätze verschiedenen Inhalts. Mit 3 Steintaf. 3.35

II. Bd.: Die Pädagogik des Kindergartens. Gedanken FR. FR.'s über das Spiel u. die Spielgegenstände des Kindes. Mit 2 Musikbeilagen u. 16 Steintaf. 3.75

—— Mutter- u. Kose - Lieder. Dichtung u. Bilder zur edlen Pflege des Kindheitslebens. Ein Familienbuch. Mit Randzeichn. in Kupferst., erklärendem Texte u. Singweisen. 4. Mit Titel in Kpfrst. u. 35 S. Noten. cart. 4.70

Frdr. Fröbel's Kindergarten. Praktisches Beschäftigungs-Spiel für Haus u. Familie. 8 Abthlgn. In buntem Carton. @ 1.00
Jede Abthlg. wird einzeln abgegeben u. enthalten dieselben :
1. Das Stäbchenlegen. Mit 1 Anleitg. u. 1000 farbigen Stäbchen zu 1", 2', 3", 4" Länge, nebst 8 Taf. m. lith. Vorlagen. 1.00
2. Die Ausstechschule. Mit Anleitg., Ausstechnadel, Unterlage u. 8 Taf. m. lith. Vorlagen. 1.00
3. Die Ausnähschule. Mit Anleitg., Stickmaterial u. Nadeln, Unterlage u. 8 Taf. m. lith. Vorlagen. 1.00
4. Die Flechtschule. Mit Anleitg., 12 Flechtblättern u. 12 Blatt Flechtstreifen, 1 stählernen Flechtnadel u. 8 Taf. m. lith. Vorlagen. 1.00
5. Das Verschränken. Mit Anleitg., e. Bündel (50 Stück) guter, biegsamer Verschränkstäbchen, u. 8 Taf. m. lith. Vorlagen. 1.00
6. Das Netzzeichnen. Mit Anleitg., Taf. m. liniirten Quadraten, Tafelsteinen u. 8 Taf. m. lith. Vorlagen. 1.00
7. Das Korkspiel. Mit Anleitg., 100 Quadrat-Korken u. den dazu gehörigen Drähten in 4 Grössen, sowie 8 Taf. m. lith. Vorlagen. 1.00
8. Das Ringlegespiel. Mit Anleitg., 24 grossen u. kleinen ganzen, u. 48 grossen u. kleinen halben Kreisen aus starkem fein lackirten Eisen-Draht u. 8 Taf. m. lith. Vorlagen. 1.00

Frdr. Fröbel's Kindergarten. Eine Weihnachtsgabe für gebildete etc. Frauen. cart. 0.65

Die Fröbel'sche Erziehungsmethode. Eine Zusammenstellung vereinzelter Mittheilungen u. Berichte. Nebst e. Kinderliede m. Klavierbegleitung. 0.65

Frdr. Fröbel. Monatsschrift für Eltern, Erzieher, Kindergärtnerinnen u. Lehrer. Organ des "Pest-Ofner-Fröbel-Frauen-Vereins." Hrsg. u. redigirt v. J. RILL u. A. SZABÓ. I. Jahrg. 1871 12 Nummern. 1.70

H. Goldammer. Der Kindergarten: Handbuch der FRÖBEL'schen Erziehungsmethode, Spielgaben u. Beschäftigungen. Nach FRÖBEL'S Schriften u. den Schriften der Frau B. v. MARENHOLTZ-BURLOW bearb. Mit Beiträgen v. B. v. MARENHOLTZ-BURLOW. 4. Mit 75 lith. Taf. Abbildgn. 3.35

—— Ueber FRDR. FRÖBEL'S Weltanschauung. Vortrag. 0.35

—— Ueber FRDR. FRÖBEL'S Erziehungsweise. Vortrag. 0.35

J. Gruber. Die Pädagogik des Kindergartens u. der Bewahranstalt. Kritisch-praktisch dargestellt. Mit 16 Steintaf. 1.05

* **Th. v. Gumpert.** Mutter Anne u. ihr Gretchen. Ein Buch für Kinder v. 4—8 Jahren u. für deren Mütter. Auch zum Vorlesen in Kleinkinderschulen u. Bewahranstalten. Mit 6 lith. u. color. Bildern in Tondr. 1.15

* **L. Hertlein.** 30 Ballspiele. Eine Anleitung zum Ballspielen m. Kindern v. 2 bis 6 Jahren sammt 30 Liedchen zur Begleitung der Spiele. Bearb. u. m. e. Vorw. begleitet. 0.65

* —— FRDR. FRÖBEL'S Bauspiele. Eine Anleitung zum Spielen u. Bauen m. Kindern v. 3—6 Jahren. Mit 22 lith. Vorlegetaf. 1.70

—— 20 Kinderspiele für kleine Kinder v. 3—6 Jahren m. Erzählungen, Erklärung, Text u. Musik. Gesammelt, erzählt u. erklärt. Mit 20 Vignetten in eingedr. Holzschn. cart. 0.85

—— Das Flechten. No. 1. Beschäftigungsmittel für Kinder v. 3—6 Jahren. Eine Weihnachtsgabe für Mütter u. Kinder. In Mappe. 4. 1.40

—— Das Flechten. No. 2. Beschäftigungs-Mittel für Kinder v. 5—8 Jahren. In Mappe 4. 1.40

—— Das Ausstechen. Beschäftigungs-Mittel für Kinder v. 3—6 Jahren. Eine Weihnachtsgabe für Mütter u. Kinder. In Mappe. 4. 1.00

—— Das Stäbchenlegen. Beschäftigungs-Mittel für Kinder v. 3—6 Jahren. Eine Weihnachtsgabe für Mütter u. Kinder. In Mappe. 4. 1.00

(s. a. Wehrenpfennig-Hertlein.)

J. Hesekiel. Die Kleinkinderschule in ihrer Bedeutung für die Arbeiterfrage. Ein Wort an alle Freunde des Volks u. der Kinder. 0.25

P. F. L. Hoffmann. Der Kindergarten in der Familie, in Spielen u. Beschäftigungen, m. erläuterndem Text nach FRÖBEL'S Grundsätzen dargestellt. Erste Serie, Heft I—XII. Mit Abbildgn. auf 108 Taf. in 4. In Etui. 2.00

Inhalt: Heft 1, 2, Stäbchenlegen in 2 Abthlgn. Heft 3, 4, Erbsenarbeiten, in 2 Abthlgn. Heft 5, Durchstechen u. Ausnähen. Heft 6, 7, Flechten m. Papierstreifchen, in 2 Abthlgn. Heft 8—12, Netzzeichnen, in 5 Abthlgn.

—— —— Zweite Serie, Heft XIII—XXIV. Mit Abbildgn. auf 108 Taf. in 4. In Etui. 2.00

Inhalt: Heft 13, 14, 15, Modelliren aus Carton; e. Modellirschule in 3 Abthlgn. Heft 16, 17, Verschränken der Stäbchen, in 2 Abthlgn. Heft 18, der gegliederte Stab. Heft 19, Flechten aus freier Hand. Heft 20, Flechten v Nippsachen. Heft 21, 22, Geometrisches Ausschneiden m. der Scheere, in 2 Abthlgn. Heft 23, Täfelchenlegen, erste Abtlg., Vierecke. Heft 24, Täfelchenlegen, 2. Abthlg, rechtwinklige Dreiecke.

Ferner ist eine *Ausgabe mit Material* erschienen :

Heft 1 enthält Stäbchenlegen. Erste Abthlg., 9 Bildertaf. m. Text u. 1000 Stäbchen. In Etui. 0.40

Heft 2. Stäbchenlegen. Zweite Abthlg. 9 Bildertaf. m. Text u. 1000 Stäbchen. In Etui. 0.40

P. F. L. Hoffmann. Der Kindergarten in der Familie, etc.

Heft 3. Erbsenarbeiten. Erste Abthlg., 9 Bildertaf. nebst Text. 800 Stäbchen u. 200 Erbsen. In Etui. 0.40

Heft 4. Erbsenarbeiten. Zweite Abthlg., 9 B.ldertaf. nebst Text, 800 Stäbchen u. 200 Erbsen. In Etui. 0.40

Heft 5. Durchstechen u. Ausnähen. 9 Bildertaf. nebst Text. 9 quadrirte Blätter. Zephirgarn. Farbenscala. Durchstechnadel, Fliespapier zur Unterlage u. 12 Blatt Schreibpapier. In Etui. 0.60

Heft 6. Flechten m. Papierstreifchen. Erste Abthlg.. 9 Bildertaf., nebst Text, Flechtnadel, 12 Flechtblätter, 540 Flechtstreifen. In Etui. 0.40

Heft 7. Flechten m. Papiersteifchen. Zweite Abthlg. 9 Bildertaf. nebst Text, Flechtnadel, 12 Flechtblätter, 540 Flechtstreifen. In Etui. 0.40

Heft 8—12. Netzzeichnen. 5 Abthlgn. 45 Bildertaf. nebst Text. 50 quadrirte Blätter, Schiefertafel m. Netz, Griffel u. Schwamm. Bleistift. In Etui. 1.20

Heft 13—15. Modelliren aus Carton. Eine Modellirschule in 3 Abthlgn., m. erläuterndem Text. 27 Taf. Modelle auf Carton gedruckt, 27 Taf. Vorlagen. Messer. Scheere. Lineal. Schneidebrett. Zirkel. Winkelmass. Eine Flasche m. Gummi u. Pinsel. In Etui. 3.00

Heft 15. Verschränken der Stäbchen. Erste Abthlg. 9 Bildertaf. nebst Text. 50 Stäbchen, 10 Zoll lang, ⅜ Zoll breit. In Etui. 1.00

Heft 17. Verschränken der Stäbchen. Zweite Abthlg. 9 Bildertaf. nebst Text, 50 Stäbchen, 10 Zoll lang, ⅜ Zoll breit. In Etui. 1.00

Heft 18. Der gegliederte Stab. 9 Bildertaf. nebst Text. Der gegliederte Stab. In Etui. 0.80

Heft 19. Flechten aus freier Hand. 9 Bildertaf. nebst Text u. 24 Blatt Flechtstreifen. In Etui. 0.40

Heft 20. Flechten v. Nippsachen. 9 Bildertaf u. auf Carton, nebst Text, u. 9 Taf. auf Carton, Pfriem, 500 Stäbchen u. Flechtstreifen. In Etui. 1.00

Heft 21. Geometrisches Ausschneiden m. der Scheere. Erste Abthlg. 9 B.ldertaf. nebst Text. Scheere. Messer 48 Blatt Papier. 60 farbige Gevierblättchen. In Etui. 1.20

Heft 22. Geometrisches Ausschneiden m. der Scheere. Zweite Abthlg. 9 Bildertaf. nebst Text. Scheere. Messer. 48 Blatt Papier. 36 farbige Sechseckblättchen. In Etui. 1.20

Heft 23. Täfelchenlegen. Erste Abthlg. Das Legen m. Gevierten. 9 B.ldertaf. nebst Text. 50 Gevierttäfelchen. In Etui. 0.80

P. F. L. Hoffmann. Der Kindergarten in der Familie, etc.

Heft 24. Täfelchenlegen. Zweite Abthlg. Das Legen m. Gedritten. 9 Bildertaf. nebst Text. 50 Gedritttäfelchen. In Etui. 0.80

F. Hüffell. Die Kleinkinderschule v. pädagogischen Standpunkte aus betrachtet. Ein Beitrag zur Beförderung des Kleinkinderschulwesens. 0.25

Jahresbericht der Kinderanstalt d. Rauhen Hauses, zugleich m. Beziehung auf das Pensionat u. die Brüderanstalt, über das Jahr 1867 (34. Verwaltungsjahr.) Mit 1 Holzschntaf. 0.25

F. Kaselitz. Gefahren moderner Jugendlectüre. Vortrag im Berliner Frauenverein zur Beförderung FRÖBEL'scher Kindergärten gehalten. 0.15

Unsere Kinder, unsere Schätze! Ein Wort an die Mütter, aus der Schule ins Haus. 0.50; cart. 0.65; geb. m. Goldschn. 0.85

* Der praktische **Kindergarten.** 1. Heft. Die Zeichenschule nach FRÖBEL's Grundsätzen bearb. v. L. MORGENSTERN. 4. 0.45

Kindergarten u. **Elementarklasse.** Hrsg. unter Mitwirkung e. Vereins v. Freunden FRDR. FRÖBEL'scher Erziehungs-Grundsätze v. A. KÖHLER, FRDR. SCHMIDT u FRDR. SEIDEL. 1.—4. Jahrgang 1861—63. @ 1.50

Die Fortsetzung bildet:

Kinder - Garten, Bewahr- u. Elementar-Classe. Hrsg. unter Mitwirkung des deutschen Fröbel-Vereins v. A. KÖHLER, FRDR. SCHMIDT u. FRDR. SEIDEL. 5. Jahrg. 1864. 1.50

—— 6.—12. Jahrg., 1865—71. @ 1.70

Die christliche **Kleinkinderschule.** Zeitschrift für christliche Kleinkinderpflege u. Erziehung für Schule u. Haus. 1. Jahrg. 1870. Hrsg. v. JOHS. BOEGEHOLD. 12 Nrn. 1.05

—— 2. Jahrg 1871. Redigirt v. ENGELBACH, GRÆVE u. WEICKERT. 52 Nrn. 0.85

Aug. Köhler. Die Praxis des Kindergartens. Theoretisch-praktische Anleitung zum Gebrauche der FRÖBEL'schen Erziehungs- u. Bildungsmittel in Haus, Kindergarten u. Schule. I. Bd. Einleitung. — Die Sinnes-, Glieder- u. Körperübungen. — Die Bewegungsspiele. — Die Bälle. — Kugel, Walze u. Würfel. — Die getheilten Würfel. Mit 18 lith. Taf.-Abbildgn. 1.70

—— Der Kindergarten in seinem Wesen dargestellt. 28 Fragen für Freund desselben beantwortet. 0.85

—— Die Bewegungsspiele des Kindergartens. Nebst e. Anhange v. Ball-, Kugel- u. Bauliedern. 1.25

—— Das FRÖBEL'sche Flechtblatt (X. Gabe). Eine Flechtlehre für Eltern, Lehrer u. Kindergärtnerinnen, welche ihre 5—10jährigen Zöglinge u. Schüler nützlich beschäftigen wollen. Mit 83 Abbildgn. 0.65

Aug. **Köhler.** Das FRÖBEL'sche Faltblatt als Anschauungs- u. Darstellungsmittel für die Schüler der beiden ersten Schuljahre bearb. u. allen Lehrern u. Kindergärtnerinnen zur Beachtung vorgelegt. Mit 65 Abbildgn. in Holzschn. 0.35

—— Die immerwährende Versetzung. Ein lebendiges Bilderbuch für Gross u. Klein. 4. 6 illum. Steintaf. m. Text. cart. 1.90

Wich. **Lange.** Zum Verständnisse FRDR. FRÖBELS. 1. u. 2. Beitrag. 0.45

E **Lausch.** 200 Kinderräthsel, Spielliedchen, Verschen u. Gebete. Für gute Kinder hrsg. 0.25

H. **Langethal.** Der erste Schulunterricht auf das Wesen u. die Entwickelung des Kindes gegründet. 0.50

G. **Lautier.** Bedeutung u. philosophische Grundlage v. FRÖBEL's Pädagogik. 0.45

* H. **Leidesdorf.** Kinderlust, oder Spiel u. Lied für Kindergarten, Schule, Haus u. Spielplatz. Unter Mitwirkung mehrerer Pädagogen hrsg. 2 Abtlgn. 1. Abthlg.: 145 Spiele m. u. ohne Gesang. 100 Reime zu Spiel u. Scherz m. kleinen Kindern. 91 Räthsel u. 37 Abzählsprüche. 2. Abthlg.: 254 Lieder m. den Singweisen, sowie e. Sammlung Reime über des Kindes ersten Verkehr m. der Natur, Kindergebete, Sprüchlein, leichte Geburtstags- u. Neujahrswünsche. 1.25

W. **Löhe.** Von Kleinkinderschulen. Ein Dictat für die Diaconissenschülerinnen v. Neuendettelsau. cart. 0.25

† * F. **Maréchal.** Rathgeber bei der Erziehung der Kleinen, insbesondere ihres Herzens. Aus d. Franz. 0.25

* B. v. **Marenholtz-Bülow.** Das Kind u. sein Wesen. Beiträge zum Verständniss der FRÖBEL'schen Erziehungslehre. 1. u. 2. Heft. @ 0.65

* —— Die Arbeit u. die neue Erziehung nach FRÖBEL's Methode. 2.10

Marienwerther Kindergärtchen für die Bewahrschule. cart. 0.45

H. **Meier.** Das Kind in seinen ersten Lebensjahren. Skizzen über Leibes- u. Geisteserziehung. Deutschen Müttern gewidmet. 0.85; eleg. geb. 1.25

W. **Middendorff.** Ueber die Kindergärten. Durchgesehen u theilweise verbessert v. WICH. LANGE. 1.05

* L. **Morgenstern.** Das Paradies der Kindheit nach FRDR. FRÖBEL's Grundsätzen. Practisches u. ausführliches Handbuch für den Selbstunterricht u. zur Benutzung in den FRÖBEL'schen Bildungsinstituten. Mit Holzschn., 10 lith. Taf. u. Noten. 1.90; geb. 2.40

* —— Die kleinen Menschen. 101 Geschichten u. Lieder aus der Kinderwelt für kleine Leser, erzählende Mütter, Kindergärtnerinnen u. Erzieherinnen. Für das Alter v. 6—11 Jahren. Mit 8 bunten Illustr. v. L. THALHEIM. cart. 1.70

* L. **Morgenstern.** Die Storchstrasse. 100 Bilder aus der Kinderwelt in Erzählungen u. Liedern für erzählende Mütter, Kindergärtnerinnen u. kleine Leser. Mit 8 bunten Illustr. v. L. THALHEIM. geb. 1.60
(s. a. "Der praktische Kindergarten.")

* **Muttersorgen u. Mutterfreuden.** Worte der Liebe u. des Ernstes über Kindheitspflege. Von e. Mutter. Mit Vorw. v. A. DIESTERWEG. 2 Bde. 1849—51. 2.50

* Th. **Naveau.** Der Kindergarten u. seine Erziehungsmittel für Jedermann fasslich dargestellt. 0.15

* —— Ausstechmappe für fleissige Kinder. 3 Hefte. 0.40

* —— Flechtmappe für fleissige Kinder. 3 Hefte. @ 0.40

* —— Nähmappe für fleissige Kinder. 3 Hefte. @ 0.40

* —— Das Legen m. Gevierttafeln. Ein Spiel für Kinder v. 5—7 Jahren. In Holzkästchen. 1.00

* —— Das Legen m. rechtwinkligen Dreiecken. Ein Spiel für Kinder v. 5—7 Jahren. In Holzkästchen. 1.00

* —— Das Stäbchenlegen für fleissige Kinder. In Holzkästchen. 0.65

* —— Frau Rosa's Kinderstube. Ein praktisches Handbuch für Mütter u. Lehrerinnen an Kleinkinderschulen. I. Thl. enthaltend: bildende Beschäftigungen für Kinder v. 3—6 Jahren, 20 lith. Mustertaf. u. genaue Anleitung zur Ausführung jeder einzelnen Beschäftigung, Beispiele zur Besprechung m. kleinen Kindern, Erzählungen, Liedchen u. Räthsel. 4. cart. 1.25

* —— II. Thl. enthaltend: bildende Beschäftigungen für Kinder v. 5—8 Jahren, in 20 lith. Mustertaf. u. e. Anleitung zum unterrichtlichen Verkehr m. jüngeren Kindern in Besprechung, Erzählung, Lied u. Gedicht. 4. cart. 1.90; 2. Thl. geb. 3.70 I. u. II. Thl. geb. in 1 Bd.

* —— Erzähl-Buch für Haus u. Kindergarten. 1. Heft. Mit eingedr. Holzschn. 0.30

* —— Neues Erzählbuch für Haus u. Kindergarten. Mit 12 eingedr. Holzschn. v. ED. ADE. cart. 0.50

* Th. **Naveau.** Aus des Kindes Heimath. 4. Mit 12 lith. Bildern, v. J. HOFFMANN. 1.90; illum. 2.50

* —— u. M. **Naveau.** 200 Spiele u. Lieder für Kindergarten, Elementarklasse u. Familie. Gesammelt u. nach Musik u. Text überarb. u. geordnet. 0.50

* —— u Fr. **Janssen.** Zeichnenschule für die Kindergärten u. für die Familie. I. Abthlg., 1. Heft. 4. Mit 5 Steintaf. 0.35

* —— 2. u. 3. Heft. Mit 9 u. 12 Steintaf. @ 0.60

H. **Nienhaus.** Geistige Nahrung für Kinder v. 4—7 Jahren. Ein Handbuch für Alle, welche m. Kindern umgehen, namentlich für Erzieherinnen u. Lehrer an Bildungsanstalten für die Jugend. Inhalt: 1. Abthlg. Sprachübungen. 2. Abthlg. Gedichtchen zum Auswendiglernen. 3. Abthlg. Spiele für Kinder. 4. Abthlg. Lieder. 5. Abthlg. Märchen, Fabeln, Erzählungen. 0.65

H. Piepenberger. Die Fröbel'schen Kindergärten. Drei pädagogische Vorträge. 0.35

H. Pösche. Frdr. Fröbel's entwickelnd-erziehende Menschenbildung. 2 Thle.

I. Theil. Die sprachliche Entwickelung u. der sprachliche Unterricht des Kindes im Kindergarten u. in der Elementarschule. Mit Zusätzen aus den Werken Frdr. Fröbel's zusammengestellt. 0.45

II. Theil. Frdr. Fröbel im Lichte der neuern geschichts-pädagogischen Entwicklung. 0.45

—— Frdr. Fröbel's entwickelnd-erziehende Menschenbildung (Kindergarten-Pädagogik) als System. Eine umfassende wortgetreue Zusammenstellung. 1.90

—— Die Ball- u. Turn-Spiele Frdr. Fröbel's. Für Haus, Kindergarten u. Schule bearb. Mit 4 lith. Zeichnungen in Tondr. nach W. Schæfer. Mit eingedr. Holzsch. 0.95

J. Fr. Ranke. Die Erziehung u. Beschäftigung kleiner Kinder in Kleinkinderschulen u. Familien. Anleitung, Kinder in den ersten Lebensjahren zu erziehen, durch Spielen, Arbeiten u. vorbereitenden Unterricht zu beschäftigen, m. besonderer Berücksichtigung der Kleinkinderschule nach der Erfahrung bearbeitet. 0.65

F. Ravoth. Ueber den Geist der Fröbel'schen Kinderspiele u. die Bedeutsamkeit der Kindergärten. Mit eingedr. Holzschn. u. 9 Steintaf. 0.50

—— Die mathematische Formenlehre der Fröbel'schen Spiel- u. Beschäftigungsmittel für Kindergärtnerinnen u. zum Verständniss der Fröbel'schen Pädagogik. Mit eingedr. Holzschn. 0.60

F. Schneyer. Beschäftigungstafeln für Kinder von 6—9 Jahren. 0.40

J. Seele. Gedichte für das erste Kindesalter zum Gebrauch im Hause, für den Kindergarten u. die Kleinkinderschule. Mit Vorw. v. H. Pösche. cart. 0.85

J. Seele. Erzählungen für Kinder v. 2—7 Jahren zum Gebrauch im Hause, im Kindergarten u. in der Kleinkinderschule. Mit Vorw. v. E. Pappenheim. Mit 6 lith. u. illum. Zeichnungen v. G. Bartsch. cart. 1.00

Frdr. Seidel. Katechismus der praktischen Kindergärtnerei. Mit 33 in den Text gedr. Abbildgn. 0.40

—— Figuren-Räthsel-Spiele für Kinder. 1. Gabe, 12 Taf. m. 119 Figuren u. 4 Holztäfelchen in Futteral. 0.75

Frdr. Seidel u. F. Schmidt. Arbeitsschule. 4.

1. Heft: Das Netzzeichnen, 1. Abthlg. (geradlinige Figuren) für Kinder v. 5—8 Jahren. 0.75

(Das Netzbuch hierzu 0.20)

2. Heft: Das Flechten für Kinder v. 3—14 Jahren. 165 Muster ohne Flechtmaterial. 0.75

Frdr. Seidel u. F. Schmidt. Arbeitsschule.

II a. Das Flechten. I. Abthlg. Für Anfänger (Kinder v. 3—8 Jahren). In einer Mappe m. 44 Mustern, farbigen Flechtblättern, breiten Flechtstreifen u. Flechtnadel. 0.50

II b. Das Flechten. II. Abthlg. Für Geübtere. (Kinder v. 7—14 Jahren). In e. Mappe m. 48 Mustern, farbigen Flechtblättern, schmalen Flechtstreifen u. Flechtnadel. 0.50

3. Heft: Das Pappen (Modelliren) für Kinder v. 8—14 Jahren. 0.75

4. Heft: Das Ausstechen, für Kinder v. 5—9 Jahren. 0.95

5. Heft: Das Stäbchenlegen, für Kinder v. 3—8 Jahren. Bearb. v. A. Köhler. 0.60

6. Heft: Die Erbsenarbeiten, für Kinder v. 4—10 Jahren. Bearb. v. A. Köhler. 0.60

7. Heft: Das Netzzeichnen, II. Abthlg., für Kinder v. 7—12 Jahren. 0.60

(Das Netzbuch hierzu 0.20)

8. Heft: Das Thonmodelliren für Kinder v. 4—14 Jahren. 0.60

9. Heft: Das Verschränken, für Kinder v. 5—12 Jahren. 0.60

10. Heft: Das Ausschneiden, für Kinder v. 5—12 Jahren. 0.75

11. Heft: Das Nähen, unter Mitwirkung v. M. Schellhorn hrsg. 1 Abthlg., für Kinder v. 4—6 Jahren. In e. Mappe m. Beigabe v. Wolle in 8 Farben. 0.80

12. Heft: 2. Abthlg., für Kinder v. 5—8 Jahren. In e. Mappe m. Beigabe v. Wolle in 8 Farben. 0.80

—— Flechtmaterial-Mappe zur Arbeitsschule II a u. II b. Enthält 2 Flechtnadeln, 72 farbige Flechtblätter u. Flechtstreifen in 3 Grössen u. 2 Breiten. 0.55

R. O. Seydler. Die Mittel der Kindergarten-Erziehung. Zweck, Bedeutung, u. Anwendung derselben. 0.25

—— Das Wesen des Kindergartens. Vortrag. 0.25

H. Stein. Das zeichnende Kind. Ein praktisches Lehrmittel zur Selbstbeschäftigung u. Uebung im Zeichnen. Ein Festgeschenk für Kinder v. 4—10 Jahren. Nach der stigmografischen Methode systematisch zusammengestellt. In Mappe. 4. 2.00

G. Steinacker. Bilder, Studien u. Klänge aus dem Bereiche des Elternhauses u. Kindergartens, der Lehr- u. Volksschule; nach Frdr. Fröbel'schen Grundsätzen. 1.25

L. Stiebritz. Allerlei Heimlichkeiten aus der Kinderstube. Bilder aus den ersten Lebensjahren. 1.05

Tante Hedwig's Geschichten für kleine Kinder. Ein Buch für erzählende Mütter, Kindergärtnerinnen u. kleine Leser. Mit 6 bunten Bildern v. L. Thalheim. geb. 1.25

Tante **Louisen's** Märchengarten. Ein Büchlein für Mütter u. Kindergärtnerinnen, artigen Kindern v. 4—7 Jahren daraus vorzulesen u. zu erzählen. Mit e Vorw. v. L. Morgenstern u. lith. u. color. Bildern. cart. 0.95

H. O. **Wagner.** Zeichnenblättchen zur Selbstbeschäftigung für Kinder. 1.—6. Heft. qu. 4. @ 0.25

* L. **Wehrenpfennig-Hertlein.** Kommt, lasst uns den Kindern leben. Skizzen über weibliche Erziehung u. Frdr. Fröbel's Erziehungs-Idee. 0.85
(s. a. "Hertlein.")

J. **Wellauer.** Ueber Kleinkindererziehung. Mit besonderer Berücksichtigung auf die Fröbel'schen Kindergärten u. ihre Anwendung im St. Gallischen Waisenhause. Eine Conferenzarbeit. 0.35

* A. **Weyrowitz.** Wer hilft der Mutter ihre erziehliche Aufgabe lösen? Vier Vorträge. 0.35

G. **Wiedemann.** Kindergärten, e. Bedürfniss der Gegenwart. 0.25

* A. **Winkel.** Das Liederbuch der Mutter. Kinderlieder zum Gebrauch im Hause, im Kindergarten u. in der Kleinkinderschule. Gesammelt u. m. leichter Klavierbegleitung versehen. 0.65

K. **Winternitz.** Lesespiel für kleine Kinder v. 4—6 Jahren, wodurch dieselben ohne eigentlichen Unterricht in entsprechend kurzer Zeit lesen lernen. Mit 100 Karten. geb. 0.85

—— Rechnenspiel für kleine Kinder v. 5—7 Jahren, durch welches dieselben ohne eigentlichen Unterricht in entsprechend kurzer Zeit mittelst der ersten 4 Rechnungsarten leicht u. auf angenehme Weise rechnen lernen. Mit 50 Karten u. Vorlegetafeln. geb. 0.85

—— Schreibspiel für kleine Kinder v. 5—7 Jahren, durch welches dieselben ohne eigentlichen Unterricht in entsprechend kurzer Zeit schreiben u. Geschriebenes lesen lernen. Mit 100 Karten. 1.70

—— Turnspiel für Kinder v. 5—10 Jahren. Mit 36 Figuren-Karten. 0.85

Der Kindergarten in Amerika. Entstehung, Wesen, Bedeutung und Erziehungsmittel des Fröbel'schen Systems, und seine Anwendung auf hiesige Verhältnisse. Für Eltern, Lehrer und Kinderfreunde kurz dargestellt. Wird *gratis* ausgegeben.

Kindergarten-Material. (Importirt.)

Beinpfriem zum Durchzeichnen.	0.12
1. Gabe: Der Ballkasten.	1.00
2. " Kugel, Walze, Würfel.	0.70
3. " 1ter Baukasten.	0.30
4. " 2ter "	0.30
5. " 3ter "	0.75
6. " 4ter "	0.75
Legespiele, Kasten mit 4 Dreiecken.	0.30
" " " 8 "	0.35
" " " 9 "	0.35
" " " 16 "	0.40
" " " 32 "	0.45
" " " 54 "	0.55
" " " 56 "	0.55
Verschränkstäbchen. 100 Stück.	0.70
Stäbchenkasten.	0.35
Der gegliederte Stab.	0.20
Kreislegespiel.	0.75
Flechtmappe.	0.50
Ausnähmappe.	0.50
Ausstechmappe.	0.50
Stählerne Flechtnadeln. ℔ Dutzend	1.20
Hölzerne Flechtnadeln. ℔ Dutzend	0.20
Carrirte Schiefertafeln. @	0.40
" kleinere. @	0.30
Bunte Flechtblätter. ℔ Dutzend	0.20
Ausstechnadeln. ℔ Dutzend	0.15
Ausstechpapier. ℔ Buch	0.40
Ausstechhefte. ℔ Dutzend	0.70
Thonbretter. ℔ Dutzend	1.20
Lithographien zur 3. Gabe, 1. Baukasten.	0.35
" " 4. " 2. "	0.35
" " 5. " 3. "	0.35
" " 6. " 4. "	0.70
" zum Kreislegespiel.	0.70
Weisse Faltblätter. ℔ 100 Stück	0.25
Farbige " (in den 6 Fröbel'schen Farben.) ℔ 100 Stück	0.25
Legestäbchen, 14½ Zoll lang. ℔ 500 Stück	0.50
Legestäbchen, 3 Zoll lang. ℔ 1000 Stück	0.30
Fröbel's grosser Körperkasten.	6.75
" 3. Baukasten, ca. 1½ Fuss hoch.	7.20
" 4. "	9.00

Vergl. auch unter *Kindergarten-Literatur:* Fr. Fröbel — L. Hertlein — P. J. L. Hoffmann —Th. Naveau—Fr. Seidel u. F. Schmidt, u. A.

Kindergarten Literature
in English, French, etc.

A. Douai. *The Kindergarten.* A Manual for the Introduction of FRŒBEL's System of Primary Education into Public Schools, and for the use of Mothers and Private Teachers. With 16 Plates, and Music for the plays and songs. Cloth. 1.00

Contents: *Introduction.* To Teachers. *Kindergarten-Games.* With 20 Songs, the text in English and German. *Gymnastic Exercises.* With 4 Songs, the text in English and German. *Mental Exercises.* 1. Childlike Songs, 23 Songs, the text in English and German. 2. Childlike Poetry without Song. 4 Pieces in English, 19 in English and German on opposite pages, 2 in German. 3. Childlike Tales, 12 in English and German, on opposite pages. *The Play of Drawing*, according to FRŒBEL's System.

Mrs. Horace Mann and **Elizabeth P. Peabody.** *The Kindergarten Guide.* Cloth. 1.25

Contents: I. Kindergarten; What is it? II. Rooms, etc. III. Music. IV. Plays, Gymnastics, and Dancing. V. The Kindergartner. VI. Kindergarten Occupations. VII. Moral and Religious Exercises. VIII. Object Lessons. IX. Geometry. X. Reading. XI. Grammar and Languages. XII. Geography. XIII. The Secret of Power. XIV. Moral Culture of Infancy.

Johann and **Bertha Ronge.** *A Practical Guide to the English Kindergarten* for the use of Mothers, Governesses and Infant Teachers, being an exposition of FRŒBEL's System of Infant Training, accompanied by a great variety of Instructive and Amusing Games, and Industrial and Gymnastic Exercises.

Numerous Songs, set to Music and arranged for the Exercises. With 71 lithographic Plates. Cloth. 2.10

Edward Wiebe. *The Paradise of Childhood.* A Manual for Instruction in FRIEDRICH FRŒBEL's Educational Principles, and a Practical Guide to Kindergartners.

This book contains 76 large double column quarto pages of letter-press, and 74 full page plates. The engravings are from German Plates that have been carefully revised and corrected by Prof. WIEBE. The work is for the use of Teachers and Mothers; it is published in 4 Parts.

Part. I. Contains First, Second, Third and Fourth Gifts, with 9 Plates. Part II. Contains Fifth, Sixth and Seventh Gifts, and 20 Plates. Part III. Contains Eighth, Ninth and Tenth Gifts, and 17 Plates. Part IV. Contains Eleventh to Twentieth Gifts inclusive, and 28 Plates. Price for the 4 Parts 3.00

J. de Crombrugghe. Les causeries de la mère. Poésies, causeries, jeux, chansonettes, airs notés, gravures et leçons pour la récréation et l'éducation du premier âge, d'après F. FRŒBEL. 4o. Orné de 50 gravures dessineés par L. Scherer, et 50 pages de musique, 4.80; bound, 6.00.

—— Le petit livre des enfants et du bon Dieu. Ouvrage couronné. Avec 25 gravures et chromolithographies par L. Scherer. 4to. 1.50

F. Frœbel. L'éducation de l'homme. Traduit de l'Allemand par J. de CROMBRUGGHE. Avec le portrait de FRŒBEL. 3.00

J. F. Jacobs. Praktisch handboek om kinderen van 2 to 8 jaren al spelende gemakkelyk en leerzaem bezig te houden, volgens de outwikkelings methode van F. FRŒBEL. Met 80 gravuren in 4to. 4.00

J. F. Jacobs et B. de Marenholtz-Bülow. Manuel pratique des jardins d'enfants à l'usage des institutrices et des mères de famille, composé sur les documents allemands. Avec 85 gravures et plusieurs pages de musique. 4.00

O. Masson. L'école FRŒBEL. Histoire d'un jardin d'enfants, simples récits pour servir aux mères de famille et aux institutrices des écoles gardiennes et des salles d'asile. Avec 18 planches gravées. 2.40

In press, to be published by E. STEIGER:

A. Douai's Series of *Rational Readers* combining the Principles of PESTALOZZI's and FRŒBEL's Systems of Education. With a systematic classification of English Words, by which their pronunciation, orthography and etymology may be taught readily without the use of new signs.

Kindergarten Gifts.
(Occupation Material.)

Gaben und Beschäftigungsmittel für den Kindergarten.

AMERICAN MANUFACTURE.

The following is a descriptive list of all the occupation material of the Kinder-Garten, with prices attached. These gifts are constructed in accordance with the German models, with such variations as have been suggested for American use. We have perfected machinery for the manufacture of the several gifts, and shall be pleased to receive from teachers, suggestions regarding any changes that may seem to them advisable.

FIRST GIFT. — For the youngest children, six soft balls of various colors. *Aim to teach color*, right and left, to develop the eye, movements of hands, arms, and feet in various plays. Per set, $1.50.

SECOND GIFT. — Sphere, cube and cylinder, made of wood. *Aim to teach form*, to notice similarity and dissimilarity of objects; sides, corners and edges of cube explained and counted; qualities and actions of sphere, cube, and cylinder different, owing to their difference in shape. Sphere viewed from all sides looks alike; but cube and cylinder present different forms, according to the manner in which we look at them, &c., &c.

The forms are neatly made by machines for the purpose, and provided with the necessary staples and holes for suspending in the air. Price in paper box per set, 75 cents. The same forms in wood box and gibbet for suspending forms, $1.25.

THIRD GIFT.—Large cube, consisting of eight small cubes. Put up in a neat wood box with sliding cover. Per box, 37 cents.

FOURTH GIFT. — Large cube, consisting of eight oblong blocks. In wood box with sliding cover. Per box, 37 cents.

FIFTH GIFT. — Large cube, consisting of twenty-one whole six half and twelve quarter cube. In wooden box, slide cover. Per box, $1.12.

SIXTH GIFT.—Large cube, consisting of eighteen whole, and three lengthwise, and six breadthwise, divided oblong blocks. In wooden box, slide cover. Per box, $1.12.

These four gifts serve as building blocks, and for this purpose — one of the most perfect, interesting, and developing features of the Kinder-Garten —there is an endless variety of plans to be carried out, one surpassing the other in interest and beauty. Lithographed plates in "Paradise of Childhood, a Guide to Kinder-Gartners" contain samples of all series of forms of life, beauty and knowledge, to be built by these blocks, as well as numerous illustrations of all other gifts.

SEVENTH GIFT.—Quadrangular and triangular tablets of colored paper board—

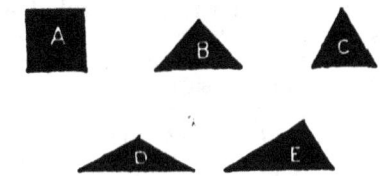

five different kinds—for laying figures. Each kind in a box. Per set, $1.25.

The same forms of tablets of wood, each form in a neat wood box with sliding cover. Five kinds as follows:

Box A 8 squares,.............	30 Cents.
" B 64 half squares,.........	75 "
" C 24 equilateral triangles colored,...........	60 "
" D 64 obtuse angled triangles,.............	75 "
" E 56 right angled 30°,.....	75 "

In the occupation with these tablets, as also in that with the material of the previous four gifts, the law of opposites, and their mediation and combination, is constantly followed. In the six previous gifts, the child had to do with solids; by the introduction of the tablets, the planes are introduced, which are followed by the introduction of the embodied straight line in the eighth gift, and the curved line in the ninth gift.

EIGHTH GIFT.—Consists of wooden staffs or wands for laying figures. As offered, these staffs are about 24 inches long, and 30 make a set. In use they are cut to different lengths by the teacher or pupils as occasion requires. Per package, 50 cents.

We prepare this gift in box containing 100 sticks cut to various lengths. Per box, 50 cents.

These staffs, as are most of the previous gifts, are employed to teach numerical proportions. That which is usually called the multiplication table is taught by means of these gifts by actual observation. Instruction in reading, according to the phonetic method, as well as imitation of all letters of the alphabet, together with Roman and Arabic numerals, are taught in connection therewith preparatory to the instruction in writing.

NINTH GIFT.—Consists of whole and half wire rings, also for laying figures. In box. Per box, 87 cents.

The rings as well as the staffs in the eighth gift are used as preparatory to the drawing occupations.

TENTH GIFT.—This gift relates to drawing, and the only material that is necessary for us to offer is paper ruled in two styles for the purpose. Put up in packages of 25 sheets in each package, ruled in squares on one side. The method by which drawing is introduced is the most systematic and perfect ever invented. It is exceedingly interesting to observe how by it even the youngest pupils will be led to perfection in a very short time. One package of each kind making 50 sheets, 62 cents.

ELEVENTH GIFT.—Material for perforating. The articles required for this gift are paper and a perforating needle. The paper is ruled the same as in the tenth gift, but is heavier so as to show the pricking better. The needle is a small handle with a point in one end. Package of paper 62 cents. Needles 12 cents each.

TWELFTH GIFT.—Material for embroidering. The embroidering is done with needles and colored silks and worsted on paper. The needles can be procured at the places where such articles are usually sold. At the commencement the same paper is used as in the eleventh gift. When the child is more advanced, paper with lithographed designs is used. The last sheets are the only articles we offer in this gift. Per set, 7 cents.

Starting from a straight line of one-eighth of an inch, the pupils produce, in course of time, the most beautiful representations of natural and artificial objects —mute, eloquent tokens of an early acquired taste in regard to form and color, and of manual dexterity and skill rarely witnessed in children of such tender age.

THIRTEENTH GIFT.—Cutting of paper, and combining the parts so produced into figures.

Squares of paper are folded in different ways, and are cut according to marks on them, by the pupils. The child's propensity to use scissors, and to destroy by using them, is here guided in such an ingenious manner, that the most astonishing results are produced.

Forty-five ruled squares of white paper and the same number of pieces ten inches square of extra heavy ultramarine paper, are put up in a portfolio, thus furnishing sufficient material to produce, mounted, the designs furnished in the "Paradise of Childhood". Price per set, as above, $1.00.

We will also furnish the ruled white papers at 75 cents per one hundred sheets. These sheets are necessarily made with the greatest care, as each piece must be exactly square and must be ruled with perfect accuracy.

FOURTEENTH GIFT.— Material for weaving or braiding. Strips of colored paper are, by means of a steel needle of peculiar construction, woven into a differently colored sheet of paper which is cut into strips  throughout its entire surface, except a margin at each end to confine the strips in place. The greatest variety of designs is produced, and inventive powers of teacher and pupil constantly increase their number.

We prepare these papers in strips of two widths, 1-8 and 1-4 inch which we designate *wide* and *narrow*, and put up in boxes. A neat box containing twelve sheets of slitted paper with a suitable number of strips for braiding, and one weaving needle, constitute a set of material. Wide, per box, 50 cents. Narrow, per box, 50 cents.

FIFTEETH GIFT. — Slats for interlacing. Thirty slats ten inches long. Per set, 50 cents.

SIXTENTH GIFT. — A set of jointed slats with four, six, eight, and sixteen links. Four jointed pieces form a set. In a box, per set, 60 cents.

SEVENTEENTH GIFT. — Paper strips for lacing.

Paper strips of various colors — eight or ten inches long, and folded lengthwise — are used to represent a variety of fanciful forms, by bending and twisting them according to certain rules. These may be prepared by the pupils, or we will supply them to order.

EIGHTEENTH GIFT. — Material for paper folding.

Square pieces of paper are here used to form variously-shaped objects by folding. The variety is endless, and the work prepares the pupil for many a useful similar manual performance in practical life. The paper must be cut exactly square. Paper cut to size in package of 480 sheets. Per package, 75 cents.

NINETEENTH GIFT. — Material for Peas-work.

Peas are soaked for twelve hours in water, and pieces of wire of various lengths, pointed at the ends, are stuck into them, for the purpose of imitating objects of life and the various geometrical figures. Skeletons are thus produced, which develop the eye for perspective drawing most successfully.

We have provided a set of one hundred wires, pointed at each end, and of assorted lengths of 1, 1 1-2, 2, 2 1-2, 3, 3 1-2, and 4 inches. In box. Per box, 20 cents.

TWENTIETH GIFT. — Material for modeling.

Bees-wax, clay or other material, worked with a small wooden knife, on a light smooth board, is used for this purpose. We do not, for the present, offer anything for this gift, teachers preferring to prepare their own material.

The materials are numbered as gifts up to 20, for the convenience of designation. But only the first six are to be used in a strictly serial order, the Planes, Sticks, Weaving and Embroidery materials, being introduced simultaneously with the third gift, so that the work of two or perhaps three consecutive days need not be alike. Variety is the spice of life in Kindergarten, and this is secured by change of material.

E. Steiger having established a

Free Bureau for suiting Kindergarteners,

and German Teachers generally

with positions, and supplying Public Institutions and Private Families with Kindergarteners, and Teachers of the

German and other Modern Languages,

begs to announce that he keeps, for the accommodation of the Public, a Record of eminently qualified persons; and he invites Kindergarteners and other Teachers looking for engagements, to send him their names and addresses, with certificates, &c. Blank Forms on application.

No charge to either Party.

Educational Publications.

Kindergarten u. Kleinkinderunterricht. Primary Education.

Der Kindergarten in Amerika. Entstehung, Wesen, Bedeutung und Erziehungsmittel des Frœbel'schen Systems und seine Anwendung auf hiesige Verhältnisse. Für Eltern, Lehrer und Kinderfreunde kurz dargestellt. Distributed gratis.

A. Douai. *The Kindergarten.* A Manual for the introduction of Frœbel's System of Primary Education into Public Schools; and for the use of Mothers and Private Teachers. With 16 Plates. Cloth. 1.00
(The text of the songs and poetry is mostly in English and German.)

Mrs. Matilda H. Kriege. *The Child, its Nature and Relations.* An Elucidation of Frœbel's Principles of Education. A free rendering of the German of the Baroness Marenholtz-Buelow. On heavy tinted paper, neatly bound in cloth. 1.00

Mrs. H. Mann and **Eliz. P. Peabody.** *Moral Culture of Infancy and Kindergarten Guide*, with Music for the Plays. Cloth. 1.25

Edw. Wiebe. *The Paradise of Childhood.* A Manual for Instruction in Friedrich Frœbel's Educational Principles, and a Practical Guide to Kindergartners. With 74 Plates. 4to. 3.00
(A very complete stock of Kindergarten Literature, in German, French, and English, and of Kindergarten Gifts, on hand. Catalogues on application.

Anschauungsunterricht.—Object Lessons.

C. Wilke. Sechzehn colorirte *Bildertafeln* für den Anschauungs-Unterricht. Mounted on 8 Boards. 5.00

Lesen.—Spelling and Reading.

A. Douai's Series of Rational Readers,

combining the Principles of Pestalozzi's and Frœbel's Systems of Education.—With a systematic classification of English words, by which their Pronunciation, Orthography and Etymology may be taught readily without the use of any new signs.

I. *The Rational Phonetic Primer.* An Introduction to the Series of Rational Readers. Boards. 0.20
II. *The Rational First Reader.* For Phonetic and Elocutional Instruction. Boards. 0.30
III. *The Rational Second Reader.* For Phonetic, Elocutional, Etymological and Grammatical Instruction. In Press.
IV. *The Rational Third Reader.* For instruction in the Laws of Pronunciation, Orthography, Grammar and Elocution. In Press.
V. *A Reform of the Common English Branches of Instruction.* Manual introductory to, and explanatory of, the Series of Rational Readers. 0.30

A. Douai. *Bilderfibel und Erstes deutsches Lesebuch.* Boards. 0.30
W. Grauert. *Zweites deutsches Lesebuch.* Boards. 0.65
—— *Drittes deutsches Lesebuch.* Boards. 0.75
—— *Viertes deutsches Lesebuch.* Boards. 1.00

These four Readers form parts of the *Turner-Schulbücher* series, intended for use in *liberal* institutions.

J. Hardter. *Erstes Lesebuch*, oder Illustrirtes Lesebüchlein für Anfänger. Ein sicherer Weg, Kinder in wenig Wochen deutsch lesen und schreiben zu lehren. Boards. 0.18
—— *Zweites Lese- und Lehrbuch* für gehobene Elementarklassen. Boards. 0.30

These two Readers are for use in schools under clerical superintendence.

Th. E. Heidenfeld. *The Phonic Speller.* Boards. 0.30
—— *First Reader.* Boards. 0.40

H. Reffelt. *Lesefibel*, oder Erster Unterricht im Lesen, verbunden mit Denk- und Sprachübungen. Boards. 0.20
—— *Das erste Lese- und Lehrbuch* für deutsche Schulen, oder: Erste Uebungen im Lesen, Schreiben und Zeichnen, verbunden mit Denk- und Sprachübungen. Boards. 0.30

H. Reffelt. *Zweites Lese- und Lehrbuch* für deutsche Schulen in den Ver. Staaten von Amerika. Boards. 0.50

—— *Drittes Lese- und Lehrbuch.* Boards. 0.70

—— *Viertes Lese- und Lehrbuch.* Boards. 0.70

—— *Fünftes Lese- und Lehrbuch.* Boards. 0.65

—— *Erstes Buch für Schule und Haus.* (For instruction in Reading, Writing, Drawing, and Arithmetic.) Boards. 0.25

—— *The same.* [With Vocabulary of all German words. For use in American Schools.] Boards. 0.30

—— *Zweites Buch für Schule und Haus.* Boards. 0.45

—— *The same.* [With Vocabulary of the German words in the first division of the book. For use in American Schools.] Boards. 0.50

—— *Drittes Buch für Schule und Haus.* In preparation.

—— *Erstes Lesebuch für Kirchen- und Sonntagsschulen.* Boards. 0.15

—— *Zweites Lesebuch für Kirchen- und Sonntagsschulen.* Boards. 0.15

—— *Drittes Lesebuch für Kirchen- und Sonntagsschulen.* Boards. 0.25

—— *Wandtafeln* für das Lesenlernen. In preparation.

——**ALPHABETICON.** (see Prospectus.)

REFFELT's Schoolbooks are based upon his 40 years' experience as a practical teacher. They are deservedly accorded the preference of all similar books published in America, and thus have a very extensive sale.

Schreiben.—Penmanship.

W. Fechner. *Systematische Schul-Vorschriften.* 6 Numbers. ℔ Dozen 1.80

Ad. Henze. *Schönschreibe-Hefte* für Schulen, nach der deutschen Preis-National-Handschrift bearbeitet. On heavy paper. 8 Numbers. ℔ Dozen 0.90

—— —— In English Script. 6 Numbers. ℔ Dozen 0.90

H. Reffelt. *Allgemeine deutsche Vorschriften* für den Unterricht im Schönschreiben. Number 1. (Copies 1 to 72.) 0.25

—— *The same.* Number 2. (Copies 73 to 144.) 0.25

Zeichnen.—Drawing.

J. Hardter. *Die Elemente des Zeichnens.* Eine systematisch geordnete Sammlung von Vorlagen. 0.25

Rechnen.—Arithmetic.

Jos. Deghuée. *Aufgaben und Anleitung zum schriftlichen Rechnen.* Deutsch und Englisch. Für deutsche Schulen in den Ver. Staaten. In 3 Parts. 8vo. Boards. Complete 1.80; or separately: 1st Part 0.80; 2nd Part 1.00; 3rd Part—for Teachers only—gratis.

H. Reffelt. *Die ersten Anfänge im Rechnen* nach der Anschauungsmethode. Boards. 0.20

—— *Kurzgefasstes Lehrbuch des Rechnens*, als Anweisung zum Gebrauche meines Rechnenbuches, sowie auch zum Selbstunterricht. Boards. 0.40

—— *Rechnenbuch für deutsche Schulen und zum Privatgebrauch.* Erstes Heft. Boards. 0.30

—— —— Zweites Heft. Boards. 0.45

—— —— Drittes Heft. Boards. 0.55

—— *Antwortenheft* zu dem Rechnenbuche. Boards. 0.36

—— *Exempelbuch für den Unterricht im Rechnen.* Erster Theil (oder 1., 2. u. 3. Heft.) Boards. 0.40

Separately:

1. Heft. Verzeichniss der in den Vereinigten Staaten von Amerika gebräuchlichsten Münzen, Gewichte und Maasse.—Einführung in das Zahlensystem und in die vier Grundrechnungen.—Die Zahlen von 1—10.—Die Zahlen von 1—20.—Die Zahlen von 1—100.—Die vier Grundrechnungsarten im Zahlenraum von 1—100. Stiff cover. 0.15

2. Heft. Einführung in das Zahlensystem und in die vier Grundrechnungen (Fortsetzung).—Die Zahlen von 1—1000.—Die Zahlen von 1—10000.—Die Zahlen über 10000. Stiff cover. 0.12

3. Heft. Die vier Grundrechnungsarten.—Addition unbenannter und einfach benannter Zahlen.—Subtraction unbenannter und einfach benannter Zahlen.—Multiplication unbenannter und einfach benannter Zahlen.—Division unbenannter und einfach benannter Zahlen.—Vermischte Exempel. Stiff cover. 0.12

H. Reffelt. *Schlüssel* zu den Aufgaben im Ersten Theile (1., 2. und 3. Heft). Stiff cover. 0.08

—— *Exempelbuch für den Unterricht im Rechnen.* Zweiter Theil (oder 4., 5. und 6. Heft). Verwandlung von ein- und mehrsortigen benannten Grössen, und die vier Grundrechnungen mit benannten Zahlen. Boards. 0.50

Separately:

4. Heft. Verzeichniss der in den Vereinigten Staaten von Amerika gebräuchlichen Münzen, Gewichte und Maasse.— Verwandlung von ein- und mehrsortigen benannten Grössen. — Resolution (Reduction descending).—Verwandlung höherer Einheiten in niedere.—(Reduction ascending).—Addition benannter Zahlen.—Subtraction benannter Zahlen.—Multiplication benannter Zahlen.—Division benannter Zahlen.—Vermischte Exempel. Stiff cover. 0.20

5. Heft. Die Brüche.—Gemeine und gewöhnliche Brüche. — Kenntniss der Brüche.—Erweitern und Kürzen oder Aufheben der Brüche.—Verwandeln des Bruchtheils einer höheren Sorte in eine niedere Sorte (Resolution). — Addition der Brüche. — Addition gleichnamiger Brüche.—Gleichnamigmachen der Brüche. — Addition ungleichnamiger Brüche. — Subtraction der Brüche. — Subtraction gleichnamiger Brüche. — Subtraction ungleichnamiger Brüche. — Multiplication der Brüche.—Division der Brüche.—Zusammengesetzte und Doppel-Brüche. Stiff cover. 0.20

6. Heft. Decimalbrüche. — Einführung in die Decimalbrüche.—Addition der Decimalbrüche. — Subtraction der Decimalbrüche.—Multiplication der Decimalbrüche. — Division der Decimalbrüche. — Verwandlungen (Reductionen).—Vermischte Exempel.—Römische Zahlzeichen. Stiff cover. 0.20

—— —— *Schlüssel* zu den Aufgaben im Zweiten Theile (4., 5. und 6. Heft). Stiff cover. 0.20

—— —— Dritter Theil (oder 7., 8. und 9. Heft). In preparation.

—— —— 10. Heft. Besondere Vortheile und Abkürzungen in den vier Grundrechnungen. — Addition.—Subtraction.—Multiplication.—Division.—Vermischte Exempel. Stiff cover. 0.15

—— —— *Schlüssel* dazu. Stiff cover. 0.08

—— —— 11. u. 12. Heft. In preparation.

H. Reffelt. *Exempelbuch für das Kopfrechnen.* Erstes Heft. Boards. 0.36

—— —— Zweites Heft. Boards. 0.45

—— *Antworten* (und Anweisungen) zu dem Exempelbuche für das Kopfrechnen. Boards. 0.45

—— *The Earliest Lessons in Arithmetic*, after the Method of Object-Teaching. Boards. 0.20

—— *The First Book of Arithmetic* for Schools and Academies. Boards. 0.30

—— *Key to same.* Stiff cover. 0.08

—— *The Second Book of Arithmetic.* In preparation.

—— *The Third Book of Arithmetic.* In preparation.

—— *The Fourth Book of Arithmetic.* Part First. Some valuable Short Methods in the four Fundamental Rules of Arithmetic. With Key to the Examples. Boards. 0.25

—— *The Fourth Book of Arithmetic.* Part Second. Equations. In preparation.

REFFELT's *Arithmetics* are extensively used; they have also been imitated, copied, and reprinted largely by German and American authors.

—— **ARITHMETICAL AID.**

—— **FRACTIONAL FRAME.**

—— **CALCULATING MACHINE.**

(see Prospectus.)

Singen.—Singing.

J. Hardter. *Kleines Lutherisches Schul-Gesangbüchlein.* Lieder und Liederverse aus dem Gesangbuch der Evangelisch-lutherischen Kirche in den Ver. Staaten. ("Das blau-goldene Buch.") 24mo. Neatly and strongly bound in boards. 0.18

H. Reffelt. *Kleine theoretisch-praktische Gesanglehre* für deutsche Schulen, mit ein- u. zweistimmigen Liedern. Boards. 0.30

—— *Deutsch-englisches Liederbuch* für deutsche Schulen. 157 ein-, zwei- und dreistimmige Lieder. Boards. 0.50

Religionsunterricht. — Religious Instruction.

E. Bohm. *Die Sonntagsschule.* Mit Genehmigung des Evang.-luther. Sonntagsschul-Vereins der Stadt New York und Umgegend herausgegeben.

Erster Cursus.	Boards.	0.15
Zweiter "	"	0.20
Dritter "	"	0.18
Vierter "	"	0.20
Fünfter "	"	0.18
Sechster, Siebenter und Achter Cursus zusammen. Boards.		0.20
Leitfaden für Lehrer. Boards.		0.12

—— *Katechismus und Sprüche, Lieder und Gebete,* sowie die Perikopen des Kirchenjahres. Zum Gebrauche in Sonntagsschulen zusammengestellt. Boards. 0.30

J. Hardter. *Erstes Lesebuch.* } see Reading.
—— *Zweites Lesebuch.* }
—— *Kleines luth. Schulgesangbüchlein.* see *Singing.*

H. Reffelt. *Erstes* } *Lesebuch für Kir-*
—— *Zweites* } *chen- und Sonntags-*
—— *Drittes* } *schulen.*
see *Reading.*

Biblische Geschichte. — Biblical History.

Zahn's *Biblische Historien,* nach dem Kirchenjahre geordnet. Boards. 0.60

Zweimal fünfundzwanzig Biblische Geschichten. (Nach ZAHN.) Ausgewählt und mit Fragen versehen von E. BOHM. Boards. 0.45

Declamation. — Recitation.

C. F. Kalm. *Deutsche Gedichte* zur Bildung des Geistes und Herzens und zur Uebung im mündlichen Vortrage. Bds. 0.50

Geographie. — Geography.

Amthor u. Issleib. *Volks-Atlas* über alle Theile der Erde, für Schule und Haus. 24 Karten in Farbendruck. 0.45. Boards. 0.90

J. Deghuée. *Geographie für Schulen.* Boards. 0.80

Globen &c. — Globes, &c.

Terrestrial and Celestial Globes, Relief Globes and Maps.

Schedler's *American Globes.*

Tellurians, Lunaria, Planetaria, &c. see *Catalogue.*

Geschichte. — History.

L. J. Campbell. *A concise School History of the United States.* Half Roan. 1.18

L. J. Campbell. *Kurzer Abriss der Geschichte der Vereinigten Staaten,* aus dem Englischen übertragen von GUSTAV FISCHER. Half Roan. 1.25

W. Grauert. *Leitfaden der Weltgeschichte.* Boards. 0.70

Deutsch. — German.

Ed. Feldner. *Kleine deutsche Sprachlehre* als Handbuch für Schüler deutsch-amerikanischer Schulen. Boards. 0.30

K. Mager. *Deutsches Sprachbuch.* Anfänge der Laut-, Wort-, Satz-, Stil- und Literaturlehre. Für untere, mittlere und obere Klassen. Paper, 1.50; Half Morocco. 2.50

A. Schleicher. *Die deutsche Sprache.* Paper 2.50; Half Morocco. 3.50

R. J. Wurst. *Kleine praktische Sprachdenklehre,* für deutsch-amerikanische Schulen bearbeitet von Director JOHN STRAUBENMUELLER. Boards. 0.50

P. F. L. Hoffmann. *Neuestes Wörterbuch der deutschen Sprache.* Boards. 1.70
Cloth. 2.00

—— *Praktisches grammatikalisches Wörterbuch der deutschen Sprache.* Cloth. 1.20

J. H. Kaltschmidt. Vollständiges, stamm- und sinnverwandtschaftliches *Gesammt-Wörterbuch der Deutschen Sprache* aus allen ihren Mundarten und mit allen Fremdwörtern. 4to. Half Morocco. 5.00

D. Sanders. Kurzgefasstes *Wörterbuch der Hauptschwierigkeiten in der deutschen Sprache.* Paper. 0.85

Lehrbücher für Amerikaner zur Erlernung des Deutschen. — For Americans, to learn German.

F. Ahn. *German Primer.* Edited by W. Grauert. Printed in large type, and with much **German Script**. New Edition, with Vocabulary. Boards. 0.45

F. Ahn. *Rudiments of the German Language.* Exercises in Pronouncing, Spelling, Translating, and German Script. With much **German Script**. New Edition, with Vocabulary. Boards. 0.50

F. Ahn. *New Method of Learning the German Language.* By Gustavus Fischer. With **German Script**. (Published 1871.) First Course, Boards. 0.50; Second Course, Boards. 0.50; Both together, Half Roan. 1.00

F. Ahn. *New, Practical and Easy Method of Learning the German Language.* With Pronunciation by J. C. Oehlschlaeger. Revised Edition of 1869. With many Reading Exercises in **German Script**.

First Course (Practical Part), Boards 0.60; Second Course (Theoretical Part). Bds. 0.40; Both together, Boards. 1.00, Half Roan. 1.25

F. Ahn. *German Handwriting.* A Companion to every German Grammar and Reader. **All in German Script**. Boards. 0.40

F. Ahn. *Manual of German Conversation.* Edited by W. Grauert. Cloth. 1.00

W. Grauert. *Manual of the German Language.*

First Part, Boards 0.40; Second Part, Bds. 0.40; Both together, Boards. 0.70, Half Roan. 0.90

W. Grauert. *First German Reader with Notes.* With much **German Script**. Boards. 0.50

W. Grauert. *Second German Reader with Notes and Vocabulary.* With much **German Script**. Boards. 0.70

The two Readers bound together. Half Roan. 1.20

H. Reffelt. *First Book for School and House.* For instruction in Reading, Writing, Drawing and Arithmetic. (In German) With Vocabulary of all German words. For use in American Schools. Boards. 0.30

—— *Second Book for School and House.* (In German) With Vocabulary of the German words in the first division of the Book. For use in American Schools. Boards. 0.50

Schlegel and **Grauert's** *Course of the German Language.* In two Parts.

Part First. *A German Grammar for Beginners.* By C. A. Schlegel. Half Roan. 1.25

Part Second. *A German Grammar for advanced Pupils.* By W. Grauert. In press.

Schlegel's *Series of Classical German Readers.* With Notes. In three Parts.

Part First. *A Classical German Reader.* With Notes and Vocabulary. By C. A. Schlegel. Half Roan. 1.00

Part Second. } In preparation.
Part Third. }

Französisch. — French.

F. Ahn. *Rudiments of the French Language.* For use in American Schools. In press.

C. Plötz. *Elementarbuch der französischen Sprache.* Nach Seidenstuecker's Methode. Boards. 0.60

C. A. Schlegel. *A French Grammar.* Part First. For Beginners. Half Roan. 1.50

—— —— Part Second. For advanced Pupils. In preparation.

C. A. Schlegel. *A Classical French Reader.* With notes. Part First. Half Roan. 0.90

—— —— Part Second. } In preparation.
—— —— Part Third. }

M. A. Thibaut. *Wörterbuch der französischen und deutschen Sprache.* Half Morocco. 3.00

Englisch. — English.

Baskerville's *Praktisches Lehrbuch der Englischen Sprache.* Gänzlich umgearbeitet und für den Gebrauch in Amerika eingerichtet von Gustav Fischer. Boards. 0.90; Half Roan. 1.00

W. Grauert. *Lehrgang der Englischen Sprache.* Erster Theil. Boards. 0.40

—— —— Zweiter Theil. Boards. 0.40

—— —— Both Parts bound together. 0.70

Wm. Odell Elwell. *Neues vollständiges Wörterbuch der Englischen und Deutschen Sprache*, umgearbeitet und vielfach verbessert. Mit Bezeichnung der Aussprache nach I. C. Worcester. 2 Parts in 1. Cloth 2.50; Half Morocco. 2.75

Deutsch, Französisch und Englisch.
German, French, and English.

A Dictionary of the German, French, and English Languages. 3 Parts in 1. Half Morocco. 4.50

Spanisch.—Spanish.

P. Henn. *Elementarbuch der Spanischen Sprache.* In preparation.

—— *A Grammar of the Spanish Language.* In prepartion.

Realkenntnisse, Naturgeschichte.
Natural History and Philosophy.

T. Bromme. Systematischer *Atlas der Naturgeschichte.* 36 Tafeln, Abbildungen und Text. Cloth. 4.00

Martin. *Naturgeschichte für die Jugend* beiderlei Geschlechts. Mit 300 colorirten Abbildungen und 20 Holzschnitten. Bound. 2.00

F. Schödler. *Das Buch der Natur,* die Lehre der Physik, Astronomie, Chemie, Mineralogie, Geologie, Physiologie, Botanik und Zoologie umfassend. Mit 976 Holzschnitten. 2 Vols. Paper. 3.30; Half Morocco. 4.90

J. A. Stöckhardt. *Die Schule der Chemie.* Mit 219 Holzschnitten. Paper 2.50; Half Morocco. 3.40

F. Strässle. Handbuch der *Naturgeschichte der drei Reiche.* Für die Jugend. Mit 32 Tafeln colorirte Abbildungen. Bound. 4.80

Gymnastik.—Gymnastics.

Ed. Angerstein. Theoretisches *Handbuch für Turner* zur Einführung in die turnerische Lehrthätigkeit. Eine Uebersicht über das Wissensgebiet des Turnens. Paper 1.90; Bound. 2.50

J. C. Lion. *Leitfaden für den Betrieb der Ordnungs- und Freiübungen.* Für Turnvereine im Auftrage des Ausschusses der deutschen Turnvereine bearbeitet. Mit 133 Holzschnitten. Paper. 0.85

Aug. Ravenstein. *Volksturnbuch.* Im Sinne von JAHN, EISELEN und SPIESS bearbeitet. Ein Führer auf dem Gebiete des Männer- und Verein-Turnwesens; auch für Turnlehrer in oberen Knaben-Schulklassen. Mit 4 Tafeln und 700 Holzschnitten. Paper. 3.00

E. G. Ravenstein and **J. Hulley.** *A Handbook of Gymnastics and Athletics.* With numerous Woodcut Illustrations. Cloth. 3.30

Für Lehrer.—For Teachers.

Hon. **Henry Barnard.** *Standard Educational Publications.* (see List.)

Hon. **Magnus Gross.** *Languages and Popular Education.* Three Addresses. (*The Study of the German Language.—The Value of Popular Education.—The Study of Languages* [with a Table showing the Pedigree of the Aryan or Indo-European Tribe of Languages].) 0.30

Suitable for Prizes, School-Libraries, Presents, etc.:

Steiger's Jugend-Bibliothek.—Steiger's Youth's Library,

being a carefully selected Series of the best writings for children, in boards, with blue and gold cover, or gray cover, with strong cloth back; 32 volumes, @ 25 Cts., have been issued, and the Series will be continued.

I keep on hand upwards of 2200 different kinds of imported **German Picture Books** and **Juveniles.** Catalogues free on application. Also sent free

Steiger's Pedagogical Library. A Catalogue of German Publications on the Theory of Education and Instruction.

All kinds of **School Books,** American and Imported, in all Languages, promptly supplied.

Free Bureau for Kindergartners, German Teachers, and Teachers of Modern Languages. No charge. Blanks sent free.

E. Steiger.

Easy and Successful
Introduction of the German Language
into Public Schools.

THE STUDY OF GERMAN
Auxiliary to the Study of English Grammar and other branches of English Education.

In the fall of 1870, the German Language became a *general* branch of instruction in the Male Department of Grammar School No. 15, NEW YORK CITY.

Of the 500 boys in the School nearly one half at that time knew nothing whatever of the German language.

When six months had expired, an examination was held to test the progress made in the new study. It was then demonstrated, in a most satisfactory manner, that though the German boys excelled the others in conversational powers, the other boys had learned the construction of the German language surprisingly well, fully equalling the German children.

The pupils not only read and translated German into English, and English into German, but also *wrote down in correct German script* English phrases given them to be rendered into German.

At the close of the exercises, Mr. Superintendent KIDDLE, congratulating the boys upon their success in engrafting the German Language on the regular course of study, made some exceedingly pertinent remarks the text of which will be found in E. STEIGER's Descriptive School Book Catalogue.

It surpassed the expectations of all present to find the *entire* class of the *lowest* grade so firmly instructed not only in pronunciation and translation but even in the correct and fluent use of German script,—and all this after barely 24 *weeks' tuition of no more than one hour and a half per week!*

The *only Text-Book* put into the hands of the youngest pupils, was AHN's *Rudiments of the German Language* (published by E. STEIGER.)

E. Steiger, New York.

Sample Type from AHN'S *Reading Charts.* (In press.)

SECTION FIRST.

The Letters, and Words of one Syllable.

in	im	Nil	nimm
in	in the	Nile	take

OBSERVATIONS: 1. **m, n, l** are pronounced as in English.
    2. Each vowel is short before a *double* consonant.
    3. *i*, when short, has the same sound as *i* in *pin, lip, bit;* *i* long, has the sound *ee* in *meet* (never like *i* in *mine*.)
    4. All nouns, common as well as proper, and words used as nouns, begin with a capital letter.

E. Steiger, New York.

First Book for School and House.
Second Book for School and House.

(For Instruction in Reading, Writing, Drawing and Arithmetic)

[In German].

WITH VOCABULARY

(FOR USE IN AMERICAN SCHOOLS).

BY

Hermann Reffelt.

First Book.	Second Book.
pp. IV, and 79. Boards $0.30.	pp. IV, and 160. Boards $0.50.

HERMANN REFFELT has had forty years' experience as a practical teacher, and his skillfully devised elementary books have in this country enjoyed a preference over books similar in kind, and have consequently had a very extensive sale. Some of his works have been imitated, copied, and reprinted on a large scale by both German and American authors.

REFFELT'S *Books for School and House* have had surprising success in German schools, and they have been found not less effective in purely American schools.

A glance at a few sample pages will suffice to show with what ease his admirable system imparts instruction in the formation of German printed and written characters,—how clearly the first elements of a knowledge of reading, writing, drawing and arithmetic are instilled into the young mind.

As in writing, from the simple upstrokes and downstrokes the letters are gradually shaped, and their growth, development, and interrelation distinctly indicated, so on H. REFFELT'S plan are drawing and arithmetic unfolded from their original elements.

Outlines and diagrams are freely used in these books, and speak to the eye in such a way, as to leave an indelible impression on the intelligence.

If ever the road to knowledge was plainly mapped out, and everything swept from it that could intercept the vision and bewilder the attention, if ever objects on that road were made to stand out so as to remain, after having been fairly scanned, forever definite to the mind, the merit of having achieved so much, by apparently such insignificant agency, belongs to HERMANN REFFELT. These *Books for School and House* discard the repulsive features of the regular Primer and by means of their simple and judicious illustrations invite the pupil to take to learning with a light heart and in good earnest.

In HERMANN REFFELT'S books we have no mere theories of instruction; whatever he puts forward has stood the test of practical experience, and results from a mature judgment. He has the happiest manner of drawing out the young intelligence; he never overburthens it, while he keeps it always in a proper state of activity. He is of vast assistance to teachers also, by his suggestiveness, his unsurpassed perspicuity of method, and his firm hold on the attention.

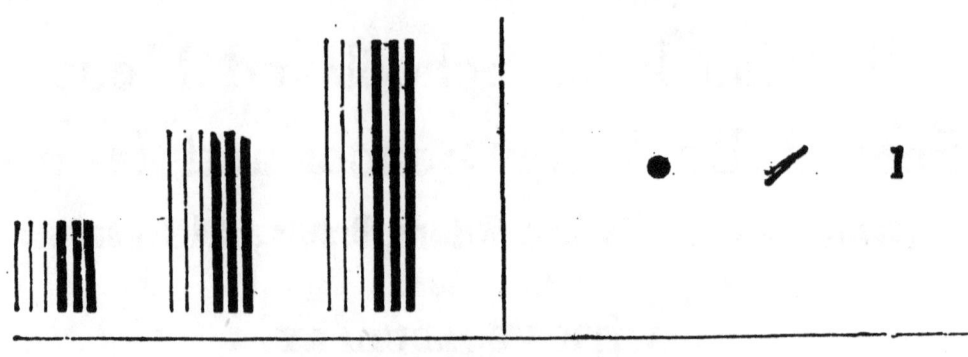

Erste Abtheilung.

I. Vorübungen im Schreiben.

1. Haarstriche und deren Lage.

1.

2. Grundstriche und deren Lage.

2.

3. Haar- und Grundstriche verbunden.

3.

4.

5.

Probeseite aus Das Erste Buch. Von H. Ressell.

— 2 —

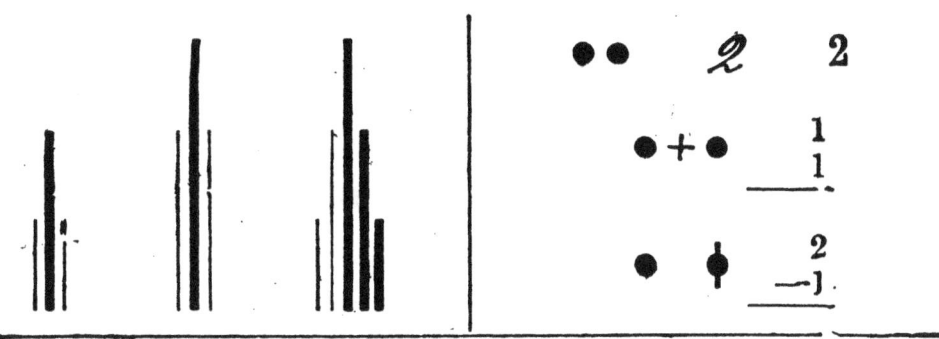

II. Die kleinen Buchstaben.

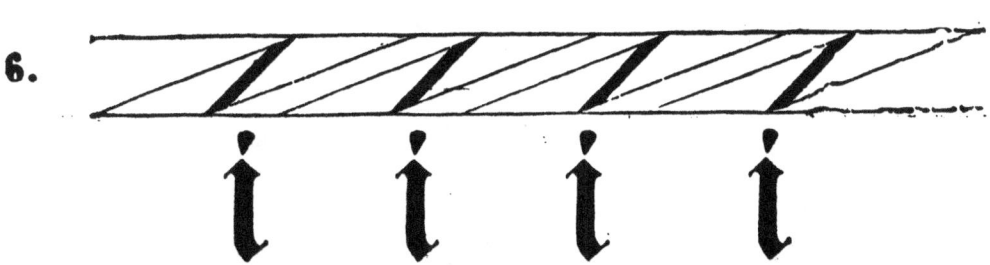

Probeseite aus Das Erste Buch. Von H. Reffelt.

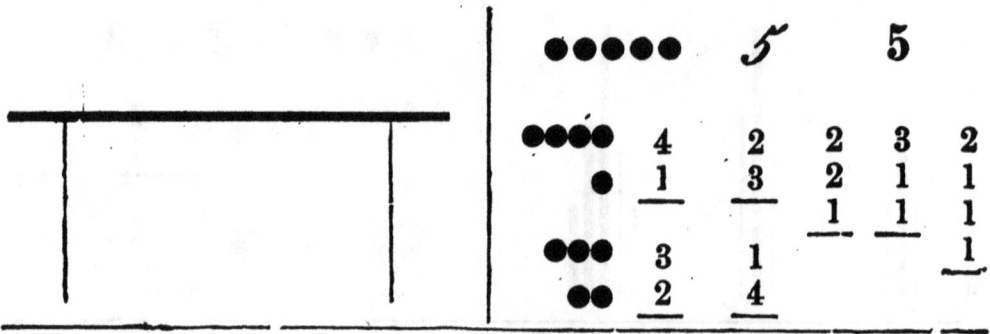

16.

o=ben, lo=ben.

be=be, le=be, lo=be, lie=be,
eb=ne, lei=me, ei=le, ei=len,
lei=men, eb=nen, lie=ben,
lo=ben, mei=nen, ei=nen,
bin, bei, ob, o=ben, je=nen,
nein, neun, mein, ein.

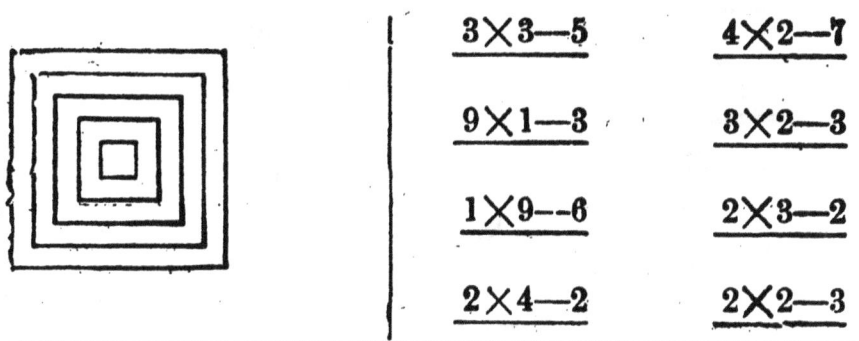

$3 \times 3 - 5$ $4 \times 2 - 7$

$9 \times 1 - 3$ $3 \times 2 - 3$

$1 \times 9 - 6$ $2 \times 3 - 2$

$2 \times 4 - 2$ $2 \times 2 - 3$

III. Die großen Buchstaben.

d D

Das Dach ist hoch.

der, die, das.

Der Daumen, die Dame, das Dach.

Der Dau=men, der De=gen, der Deich, der Don=ner, der Dom; die Dame, die Do=se, die Dau=er, die Di=na, die Do=ris; das Dach, das Dös=chen, das Däum=chen, das Däm=chen. Die Dau=ne, die Di=stel, der Dieb, die Die=le,

— 55 —

10	9	8	7	12
7	8	9	10	5
13	6	3	4	15
4	11	14	13	2

59.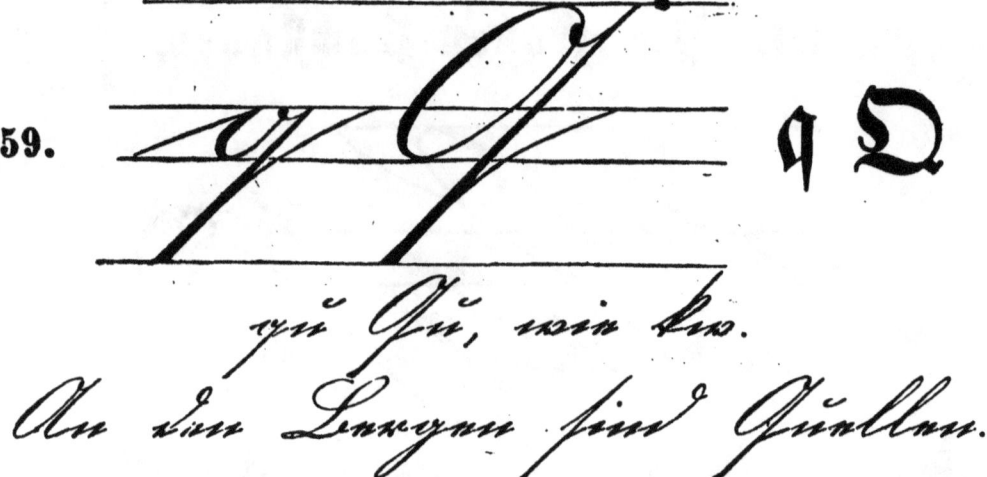

Der Quäker, der Qualm, das Quadrat, die Qual, die Quappe, das Quartier, das Quartal, der Quarz, die Quecke, das Quecksilber, die Quelle, die Quinte, die Quittung, die Quitte, quer, quaken, quälen, quellen, quittiren, erquicken.

Drei Monate machen ein Quartal. Das Quadrat hat vier Ecken. In der Quelle ist Wasser. In dem Acker sind oft viele Quecken. Das Quecksilber ist flüssig. Die Frösche quaken. Die Quitten sind gelb. Was ist ein Querkopf? Quäle keine Thiere. Was erquickt den Durstigen? Was ist eine Quittung? Der Quarz ist hart. Der Knabe hat seinen Finger gequetscht. Die Lampe qualmte. Das Schwein quiekte.

Probeseite aus **Das Zweite Buch**. Von H. Reffelt.

E. Steiger, New York.

Reffelt's Arithmetical Aid,

Patented March 3d, 1863.

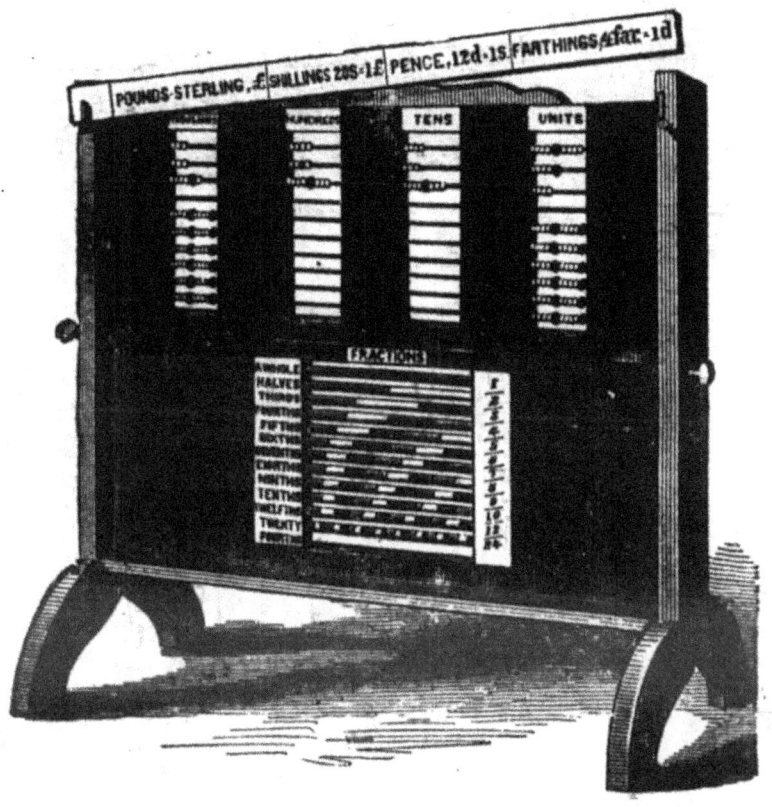

For Teaching

*Numeration and Notation,
Addition,
Subtraction,
Multiplication,
Division,
Weights, Measures and Currency,
Mental Arithmetic,
Fractions, etc.*

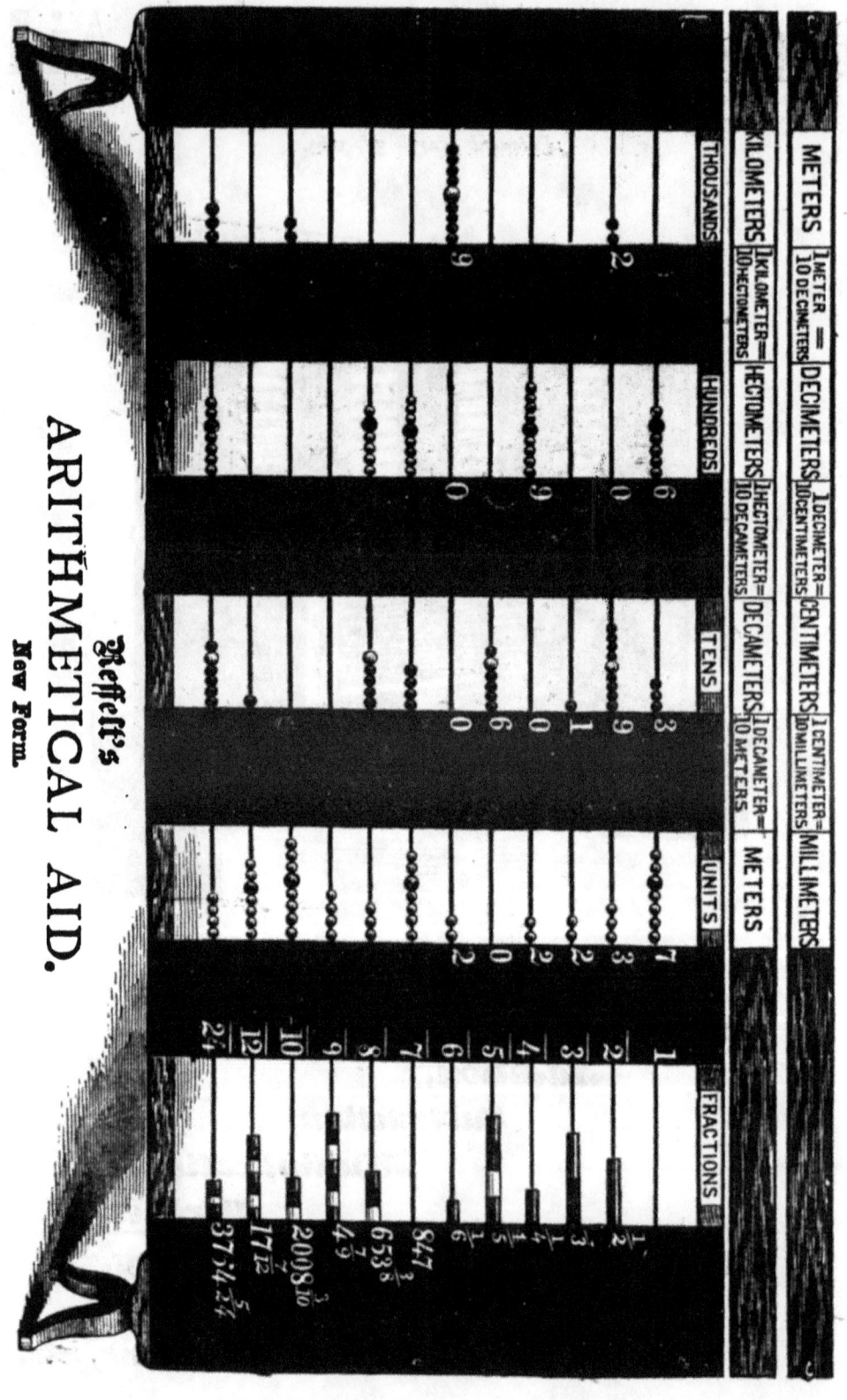

REFFELT'S FRACTIONAL FRAME.

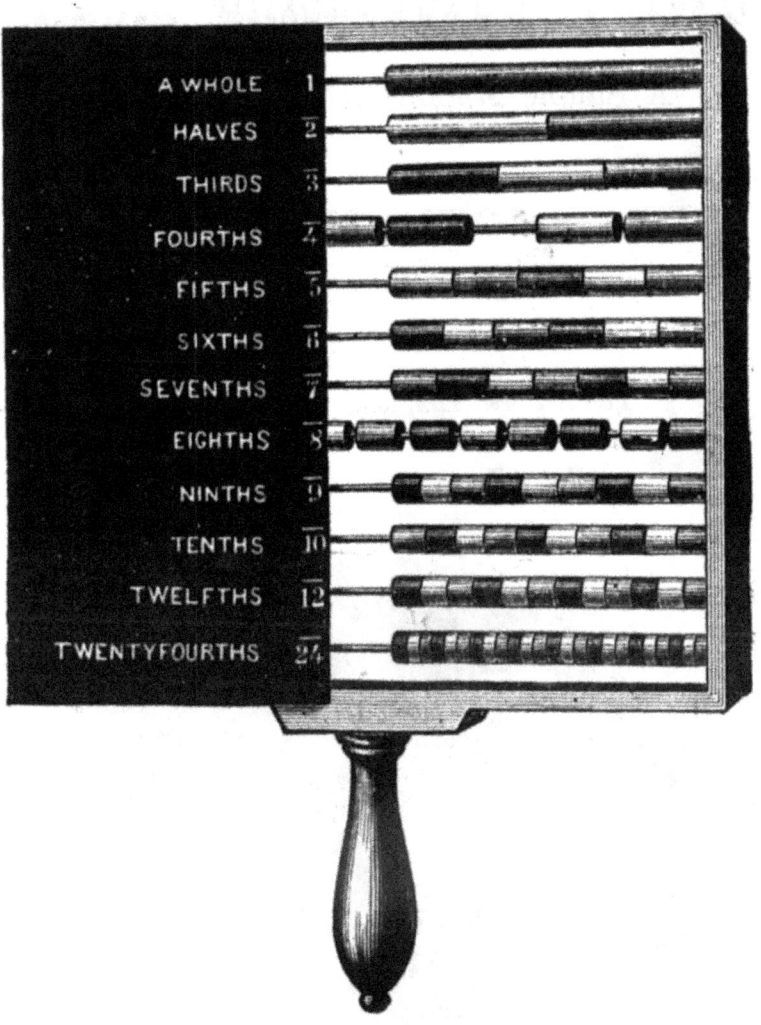

PRICES.

Reffelt's Arithmetical Aid.	Original Form.	5½ ft. × 4½ ft.	$20.00
		Packing, extra	3.00
do.	do.	4½ ft. × 3½ ft.	15.00
		Packing	2.00
do.	New Form.	5 ft. × 1¼ ft.	12.00
		Packing	1.25
Reffelt's Fractional Frame,	separate.	14 × 13 inches	4.00
		Packing	0.50

E. Steiger, New York.

Reffelt's Calculating Machine.

A Simple Machine that will perform

ADDITION,
SUBTRACTION,
MULTIPLICATION, and
DIVISION.

Patented Sept. 14th, 1869, by J. H. R. Reffelt.

Fig. 1

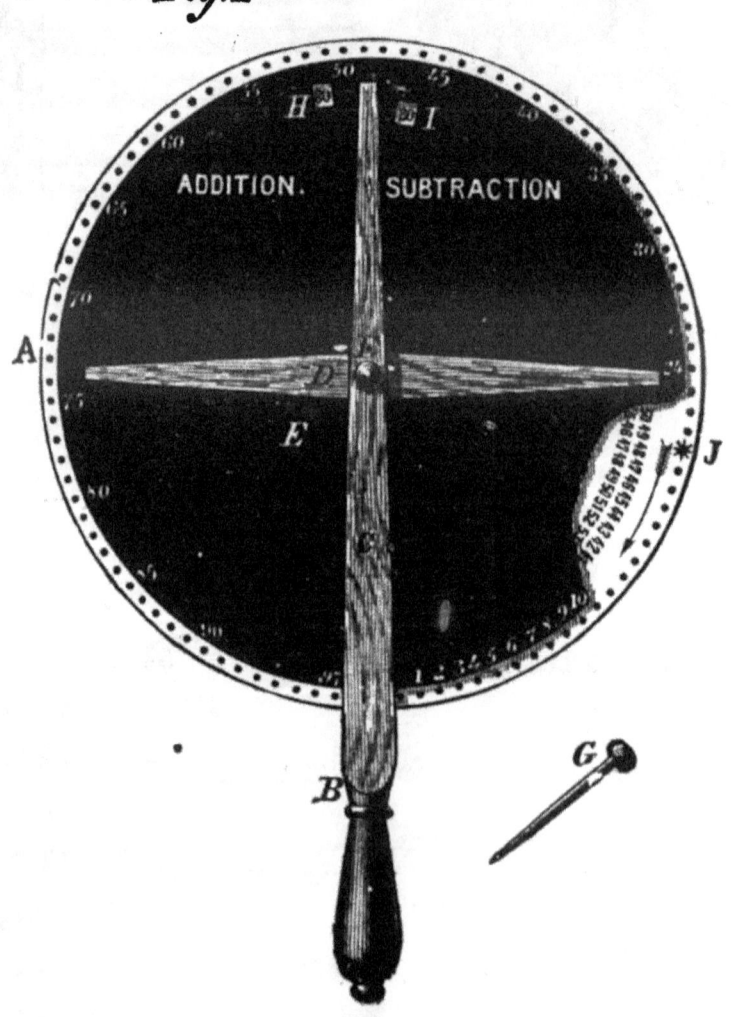

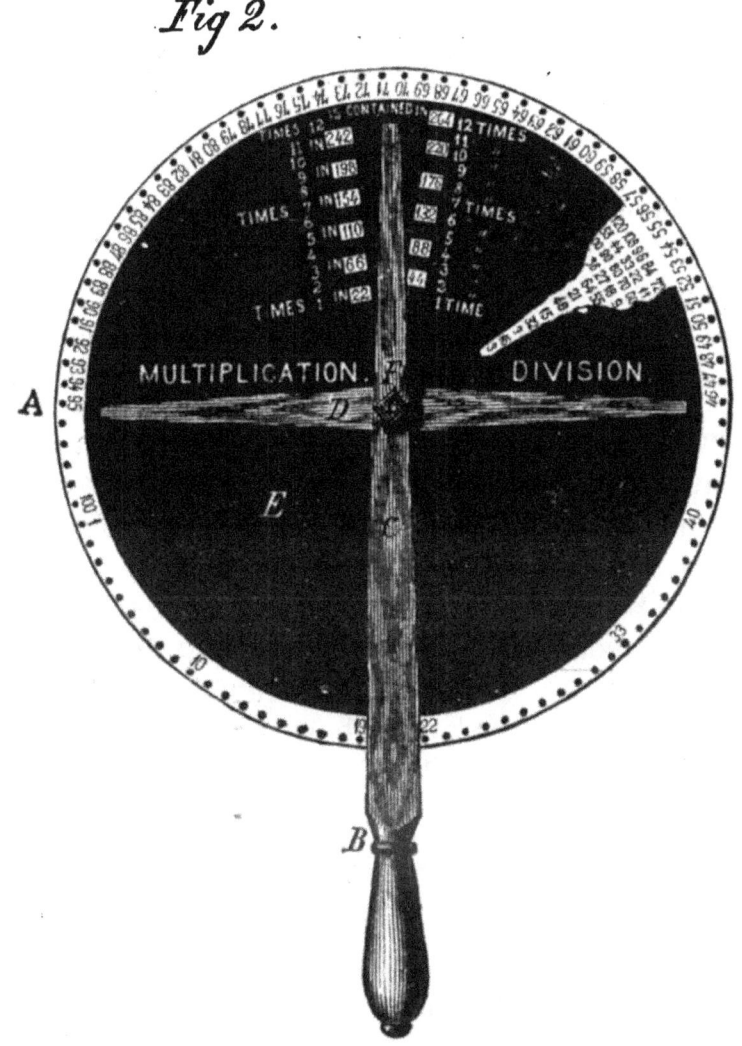

Fig 2.

☞ The CALCULATING MACHINE of simple construction—as shown above—(Price $3.00) is adapted *for use in Schools.*

A more complete style is manufactured *for business purposes,* by which 1 to 6 rows of figures may be readily dealt with at once. Price $5.00.

Liberal Terms to Schools, to Agents and Canvassers.

E. Steiger.

H. Reffelt's
Calculating Machine in the School-Room.

In proportion to the advances of Science, the labors of both the teacher and the pupil have increased. Various efforts have consequently been directed, at one and the same time, to an improved system of tuition, and a diminution of its toils, for the advantage alike of the professor and the scholar.

This twofold object has not, however, been practically achieved in every instance, for it has too often happened that an improved method of teaching, while benefitting the pupil, has accumulated difficulties in the path of the teacher. In times like the present, the instructor is taxed to the utmost,—indeed not uncommonly beyond his physical and mental strength. Plans are, therefore, in requisition to ease the labor principally of the teacher and subordinately of the pupil; and among the most successful, Mr. Reffelt's recently invented Calculating Machine establishes an incontestable claim to ingenuity and usefulness, as an invaluable aid to instruction in Mental Arithmetic.

By the use of this Machine, the teacher can make the pupil *add*, *subtract*, *multiply* and *divide*, without himself testing every petty detail involved in such calculations; for while presenting the problem to the pupil, he has to look only to the Machine for its solution. Thus, should he wish a column of figures to be added up mentally, he calls out the numerals to the pupil, and, when he calls out the last numeral, the infallible answer stands registered before him.

To illustrate the extreme ease and simplicity with which the Machine operates, let the teacher, blindfold if he likes, insert the style in any hole, which may *e. g.* chance to be at 14; let him call out this corresponding number (14) to the pupil, and then bring the style, inserted in the hole, down against the bar to zero;—next let him re-insert the style, perchance, at 16, calling out that number to be added to the foregoing, and bringing the hole down to zero;—lastly let him again insert the style, say, at 15, repeating the previous process:—the instant he has done so, the Machine will register the correct total = 45, without any more labor on the part of the teacher. And so on with any numerals selected or taken at random; the teacher utters his word of command, and by a simple manipulation the Machine obeys and registers invariably the true result.

In this simple and certain manner, the teacher has the *great advantage* of sparing himself all exertion whatever in that mental calculation which belongs to the pupil, and he can devote the time and labor so economized to a closer attention to discipline; *while his intellectual faculties not having been called into play, are as fresh and as free as at starting, to enter upon a succeeding lesson.* Young teachers, in particular, who have not yet acquired sufficient facility and certainty in Mental Arithmetic, will find this Machine a great *desideratum*.

With equal ease and inerrancy, this Machine is adapted to *subtraction*, *multiplication* and *division*, as is shown in a readily intelligible explanation printed on the disks; and as a 'Ready Reckoner' it will prove a boon in every counting-house.

To expatiate on the manifold advantages of the Machine, would carry us beyond due limits: a trial would soon make them manifest to every teacher. The Inventor, having himself had thirty-seven years' successful experience in education, may be presumed fully to understand whatever is most needed and best adapted to educational purposes.

THE CALCULATING MACHINE is, therefore, confidently recommended to *all teachers;* its use would in a very short time demonstrate how effectually and readily their task may be lightened, and the interest of their important calling promoted.

J. SCHEDLER'S
American Globes

were awarded the First Class Prize Medal at the Paris Exhibition, 1867, and at the New York American Institute Fair, 1869. They have been introduced into the Public Schools of New York, St. Louis, Detroit, and many other Cities.

More than ten years' study has been devoted to bringing these Globes to their present state of perfection. The Maps are not a mere reduction of previously existing maps, but are carefully compiled and constructed on scientific principles. The latest and most important geographical discoveries, as soon as they are authenticated, are engraved on the plates, and several maps have been repeatedly re-engraved so as to present a faithful delineation of the current state of geographical knowledge.

The mode of manufacturing the globe itself is an invention secured by Letters Patent, Nov. 24th, 1868.

By this process are ensured a perfectly spherical form, great strength and durability; and the globes are not only not liable to get broken, but they can be produced at a low price.

These Globes are beautifully printed in colors,—the water blue, which besides being more natural than white shows up the ocean currents as well as the land far more distinctly. Another advantage of this arrangement is that the color does not soil or look old so soon as white.

Mr. J. Schedler personally superintends the manufacture of his Globes, and none are sent out until they have been strictly examined and approved by him. Nearly all styles are mounted on elegant bronzed cast iron frames or stands. These are handsome, durable, liable neither to break nor shrink, withstanding the influence of temperature and climate; and they are too heavy to be easily upset.

The single parts of the globes, horizon, meridian, hour-circle and quadrant, coincide exactly.

Old globes can be remounted with new maps, and the fixtures cleaned equal to new, at a trifling cost.

J. Schedler's American Globes.

TERRESTRIAL GLOBES, OF 20 INCHES DIAMETER.
Scale 1 : 25,000,000.

The Prices within brackets [ ] denote the extra cost of *packing*.

I. The Parlor Globe.
A beautiful ornament to the Parlor or Library.

Schedler's Globe. I A.   The Parlor Globe.

A. Complete. On fine bronze pedestal frame, 42 inches high. With horizon, brass meridian divided in half-degrees, hour-circle, quadrant, and magnetic needle. $175.00 [5.00]

A 1. Complete. On low frame of black polished wood, with brass fixtures. 80.00 [4.00]

II. The Scientific Globe.

Schedler's Globe.
II A. and III A

The Scientific
and School Globe.

This is the most perfect Globe ever produced. Not only has the closest attention been bestowed on the latest and most authentic discoveries made in different parts of the world, but a great variety of information on interesting physical matters will be found on it.

It contains the Lines of *Oceanic Steam Communication* and *Overland Routes*; the great aërial and submarine *Telegraph Lines* and the principal *Tracks of sailing Vessels*; showing the directions and mean *velocity* of the

Oceanic Currents, important *Deep Sea Soundings*, also the lines of equal *Magnetic Variations*.

Schedler's Globe. II B. and III B.

The Scientific and School Globe.

A. Complete. On bronzed pedestal frame, 42 inches high. With horizon, (cast iron, nickel-plated) meridian divided in half-degrees, hour-circle, and quadrant.   75.00 [5.00]
(With brass meridian 15.00 extra.)

B. With full meridian. On bronzed pedestal frame, with full (cast-iron) meridian, and inclined axis.   60.00 [4.00]

C. Plain. On plain iron stand.   55.00 [4.00]

III. The School Globe.

In size, form and fixtures, this Globe is similar to the Scientific Globe. It is specially prepared for the use of Colleges and Schools. Objects, notwithstanding their multiplicity, are kept clear and distinct, and all confusion is avoided. Thus it readily elucidates those fundamental and elementary principles in geography, so difficult to the comprehension of the learner. The most important rivers, capital cities, and mountain ranges, are given in a very manifest and striking manner. The Globe therefore commends itself to parents and teachers as an essential aid in instruction. Its practical utility cannot fail to be recognized in Schools; it has already been received with great favor by eminent instructors in many of our Normal and High Schools, who have earnestly testified to its value; and it may be confidently put forward as better calculated for the instruction of youth than any Terrestrial Globe hitherto constructed.

A. Complete. On bronzed pedestal frame, 42 inches high. With horizon, (cast-iron, nickel-plated) meridian divided in half-degrees, hour-circle and quadrant. 65.00 [5.00]

B. With full meridian. On bronzed pedestal frame, with full meridian, and inclined axis. 50.00 [4.00]

C. Plain. On plain iron stand. 45.00 [4.00]

☞ Special wishes in regard to coloring, fixtures, etc., will be complied with, if practicable.

Celestial Globes, OF 20 INCHES DIAMETER, in same styles, and at same prices, are in preparation.

IV. Terrestrial and Celestial Globes, OF 16 INCHES DIAMETER, are in preparation.

V. Terrestrial Globes, OF 12 INCHES DIAMETER.

Beautifully printed in colors, the water blue, the ocean currents white, indicating the principal lines of Oceanic Steam Communication, and the Submarine Telegraph Cables.

A. Complete. On low bronzed frame, with horizon, meridian, hour-circle and quadrant. 25.00 [2.50]

B. With full meridian. On bronzed stand, with full meridian, and inclined axis. 18.00 [2.00]

C. Plain. On low bronzed iron stand, with inclined axis. 15.00 [2.00]

Celestial Globes, OF 12 INCHES DIAMETER, in same styles, and at same prices, are in preparation.

Terrestrial Globes, OF 12 INCHES DIAMETER.

V B.

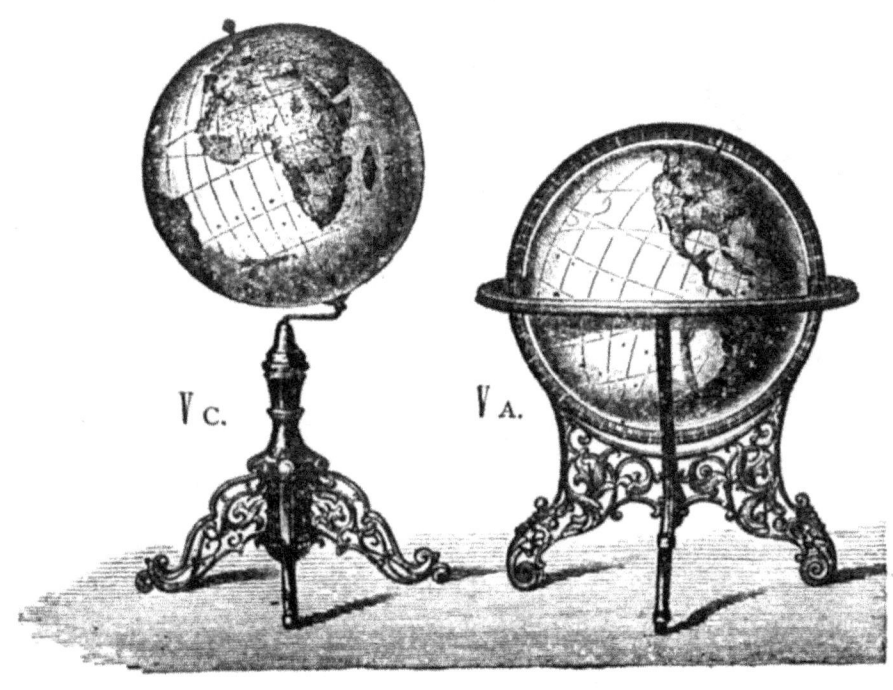

V C.   V A.

J. Schedler's American Globes.

VI. *Terrestrial Globes,*
OF 9 INCHES DIAMETER.

A. Complete. On low iron frame, with horizon, meridian, and hour-circle.   16.00 [1.80]

B. With full meridian. On low iron stand, with full meridian, and inclined axis.   12.00 [1.20]

C. Plain. On plain iron stand.   9.00 [1.00]

Celestial Globes, OF 9 INCHES DIAMETER, are in preparation.

VII. *Terrestrial Globes,*
OF 6 INCHES DIAMETER.

A. Complete. On low iron stand, with horizon, meridian, hour-circle, and quadrant.   10.00 [0.60]

B. With full meridian. On low iron stand, with full meridian, and inclined axis.   5.00 [0.50]

C. Plain. On low iron stand, with inclined axis.   4.00 [0.40]

D. In Paper Box. (The Globe when used to be put on the top of the Box.)   3.00 [0.40]

VIII. *Terrestrial Globes,*
OF 4 INCHES DIAMETER.

B. With full meridian. On low iron stand, with full meridian, and inclined axis.   3.50 [0.40]

C. Plain. On low iron stand, with inclined axis.   3.00 [0.30]

D. In Paper Box. (The Globe when used to be put on the top of the Box.)   2.50 [0.30]

IX. Terrestrial Globes,
OF 3 INCHES DIAMETER.

IX B.   IX D.

B. With full meridian. On low iron stand, with full meridian, and inclined axis.   2.50   [0.30]

C 1. Plain. On iron stand.   1.50   [0.30]

C 2. Plain. On neat low iron stand, to be used as desk-weight.   1.50   [0.25]

D. In Paper Box. (The Globe when used to be put on the top of the Box.)   1.50   [0.25]

NOTICE. **Slate Globes** of all the different sizes are in preparation, and will soon be ready.

TESTIMONIALS.

I have examined Mr. J. Schedler's 'American Globes'. The best geographical positions seem to be used, and the most recent discoveries are given. The great currents of the ocean, and the principal routes by Steamers are indicated. As maps they are neatly drawn, of names very full, the writing being clear and distinct.
         C. H. F. PETERS,
         Professor of Astronomy and Mathematics, Hamilton College.

I have examined with Prof. Hilgard, of the Coast Survey, the 20-inch Terrestrial Globe by J. Schedler, and I have no hesitation in commending it to all who desire a superior article of the kind. It is not surpassed by the best Globes of European manufacture.
         HENRY BARNARD,
         Commissioner of Education, Washington, D. C.

The Terrestrial Globe by J. Schedler we regard as invaluable. As an object of art it is really beautiful, and for scientific study could hardly be improved.
         S. M. CAPRON,
         Principal High School, Hartford.

I am much pleased with the 20-inch Schedler Globe. In modern additions to Geography, in all political changes, it takes precedence of all other Globes I know. The style of engraving and coloring is distinct and pleasing.
         Prof. J. E. HILGARD,
         U. S. Coast Survey Office.

In this Globe by J. Schedler, we find not only the utmost regard paid to the latest geographical discoveries, but also a variety of important, accurate and valuable information on physical matters. Mr. Schedler has introduced on his Globe, without prejudice to its clearness, a surprisingly large number of names.
         Prof. ROBERT SCHLAGINTWEIT, New York.

Imported GLOBES, MAPS, etc.

The Prices within brackets [ ] denote the extra cost of *packing*.

Relief Globes, of 12 Inches Diameter.

Fig. 1.

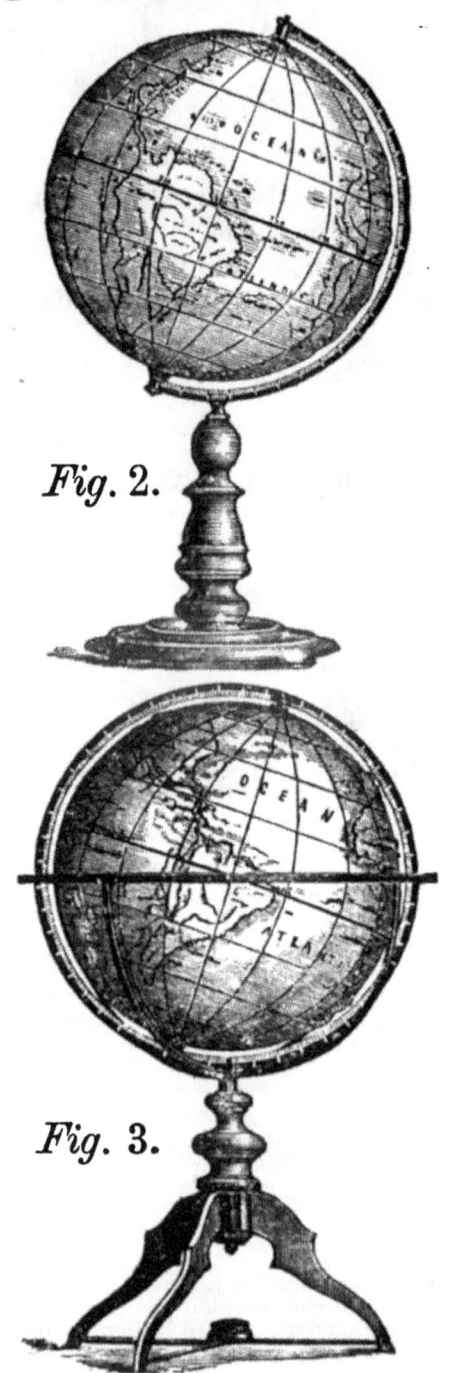

Fig. 2.

Fig. 3.

No. 0a. Relief Terrestrial Globe, with names in English, political divisions, ocean-currents, on stand of black polished wood. (Fig. 1.) $17.00. [2.00]

No. 0b. The same, with graduated brass half-meridian. (Fig. 2.) 20.75. [2.00]

No. 0c, The same, with horizon, astronomical disk, graduated brass meridian, hour-circle, quadrant and compass. (Fig. 3.) 33.00. [2.50]

IMPORTED GLOBES, MAPS, etc.

Relief Globes, of 16 Inches Diameter.

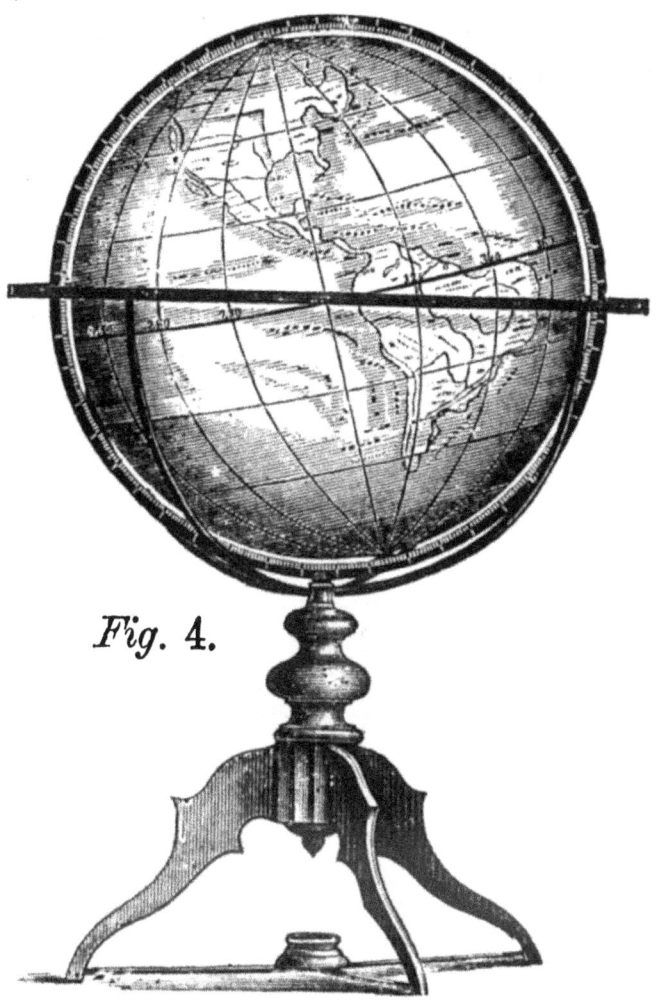

Fig. 4.

No. 1. **Relief Terrestrial Globe,** for Primary Schools and the Blind, without names, completely reticulated to represent the degree and river systems, on stand of black polished wood. (like Fig. 1.) 16.00. [3.00]

No. 4. **Relief Terrestrial Globe,** fully and distinctly lettered in English, without political divisions (each continent differently colored) with ocean-currents, completely reticulated to represent the degree and river systems, on stand of black polished wood, (like Fig. 1.) 25.00. [3.00]

No. 5. The same, with graduated brass half-meridian. (like Fig. 2.) 32.00. [3.00]

No. 8. The same, with horizon, astronomical disk, graduated brass meridian, hour-circle, quadrant and compass. (Fig. 4.) 45.00. [4.00]

No. 24. **Relief Terrestrial Globe,** with full lettering in English, political divisions and ocean-currents, on stand of black polished wood. (like Fig. 1.) 24.00. [3.00]

IMPORTED GLOBES, MAPS, etc.

No. 25. **Relief Terrestrial Globe**, with graduated brass half-meridian. (like Fig. 2.) 32.00. [3.00]

No. 28. The same, with horizon, astronomical disk, graduated brass meridian, hour-circle, quadrant and compass. (Fig. 4.) 48.00. [4.00]

*No. 44. The same after Von Sydow, with full lettering, oro-hydrographic divisions, ocean-currents, on stand of black polished wood. (like Fig. 1). 24.00. [3.00]

*No 45. The same, with graduated brass half-meridian. (like Fig. 2.) 32.00. [3.00]

*No 48. The same, with horizon, astronomical disk, graduated brass meridian, hour-cirle, quadrant and compass. (Fig. 4.) 48.00. [4.00]

* On the Relief Terrestrial Globe after Von Sydow, the elevations are colored brown, the level surfaces white, and the depressions green. This Relief Globe is the same as No. 24, 25 and 28.

Relief Globes, of 26 Inches Diameter.

A fine Globe for High Schools and Amateurs, on handsome black polished tripod with brass casters.

No. 64. **Relief Terrestrial Globe,** with political divisions, ocean-currents, complete in detail. 80.00 [6.00]

No. 65. The same, with movable graduated brass half-meridian. 100.00. [6.00]

No. 67. The same, with horizon, astronomical disk (the constellations in relief on metal) graduated brass meridian, hour-circle, quadrant and compass. 150.00. [9.00]

Relief Globes, of 48 Inches Diameter.

"THE MAMMOTH GLOBE."

A masterpiece of workmanship. On most handsome black polished pedestal frame with brass casters,—the Globe supported on three superbly gilt dolphins.

No. 80. **Relief Terrestrial Globe** (the elevations in the proportion of 10 : 1, as to superficial length) with political divisions, ocean-currents, and very complete in detail. 300.00. [15.00]

No. 81. The same, with horizon, astronomical disk (the constellations in relief on metal), graduated brass meridian, hour-circle, quadrant and compass. 500.00. [22.50]

IMPORTED GLOBES, MAPS, etc.

Relief Maps, fully and distinctly lettered
(in German, unless otherwise stated).

In superior oil-colors, with political divisions differently colored, reticulated to represent the degree and river systems, complete in details, varnished. In elegant frames, highly ornamental.

No. 88.	Relief Map of Germany, 28x28".	15.20.	[1.00]
No. 92.	" " Austria, 24x31".	13.30.	[1.00]
No. 96.	" " Russia in Europe, 25x22".	13.30.	[1.00]
No. 104.	" " France, 21x23". (Names in French.)	13.30.	[1.00]
No. 109.	" " Italy, 21x23". (Names in Italian.)	13.30.	[1.00]
No. 116.	" " Palestine, 22x17".	8.00.	[1.00]
No. 117a, 117b.	Relief Map of Eastern and Western Hemisphere, 20x22", 2 Maps,	each 8.00.	[1.00]
No. 118.	Relief Map of Switzerland, 30x24½".	13.30.	[1.00]
No. 124.	" " England, 22x18".	13.30.	[1.00]
No. 132.	" " Sweden and Norway, 22½x27½". (Names in Swedish).	13.30.	[1.00]
No. 134.	" " Europe, 20x24".	13.30.	[1.00]
No. 139.	" " Asia, 20x24".	13.30.	[1.00]
No. 143.	" " North America, 20x24".	13.30.	[.100]
No. 147.	" " South America, 20x24".	13.30.	[1.00]
No. 151.	" " Africa, 20x24".	13.30.	[1.00]
No. 155.	" " Australia and the Australasian Islands, 20x24".	13.30.	[1.00]
No. 186.	" " Jerusalem, in fine rosewood frame, 12x9".	8.00.	[0.60]
No. 186a.	" " " in paper box.	5.30.	[0.60]

Suitable for Cabinet use and Schools.

Ravenstein's Relief Atlas,

containing **Relief Maps** of North America, South America, Europe, Asia, Africa, Australia and Germany, presenting to view an actual picture of Physical Geography. Sixteen Maps colored, eight of which in relief depict the superficial character of the Earth. In case, with ornamental title.   5.00

Relief Map of the United States,

Mexico, Cuba, Canada, etc. Edited by Rev. W. L. GAGE.   1.50.

IMPORTED GLOBES, MAPS, etc.

Relief Map of Palestine,

With **Relief Plan** of Jerusalem.   Edited by Rev. W. L. GAGE.
    1. Old Testament era.   1.00
    2. New Testament era.   1.00

These 2 maps represent the Holy Land as it was, and as it is, exhibiting the hills, mountains, valleys, etc., in their exact appearance. Their size conforms to the needs of the Sabbath School Class; yet the maps will make pleasant pictures for walls of a study. The colors interpret the character of the soil. The highest elevation represented (Hermon) being 10,600 feet, other mountains are of proportionate altitude.

Relief Map of the Sinaitic Peninsula,

With **Relief Plans** showing the migration of Abraham, and the Sinai-
    Group.   Edited by Rev. W. L. GAGE.   1.50

☞ The elegance of these maps may be much enhanced by enclosing them in a neat gilt or black walnut and gilt frame with or without glass.

Indestructible Plain Globes.   COLORED AND VARNISHED.

        a) **Terrestrial.**

    1. *On stand of black polished wood.*

No.					Price	[Disc.]
No. 188.	Terrestrial Globe,	1½	inches	Diameter.	0.40.	[0.25]
No. 189.	"	2	"	"	0.60.	[0.25]
No. 190.	"	3	"	"	0.90.	[0.30]
No. 191.	"	5	"	"	1.50.	[0.40]
No. 192.	"	7	"	"	3.30.	[0.65]
No. 193.	"	9	"	"	5.50.	[0.80]
No. 194.	"	12	"	"	7.50.	[1.20]
No. 194b.	"	20	"	"	24.00.	[3.00]

Toy Globe, 1 inch Diameter, 40 cents each.   ℔ doz. 3.00.

IMPORTED GLOBES, MAPS, etc.

II. *With graduated brass half-meridian.*

No. 195.	Terrestrial Globe, 3 inches Diameter.	1.75.	[0.30]
No. 196.	" " 5 " "	2.90.	[0.40]
No. 197.	" " 7 " "	5.30.	[0.65]
No. 198.	" " 9 " "	8.20.	[0.80]
No. 199.	" " 12 " "	11.50.	[1.20]
No. 199b.	" " 20 " "	32.00.	[3.00]

III. *With horizon, graduated brass full meridian, hour-circle, quadrant and compass.*

No. 212.	Terrestrial Globe, 7 inches Diameter.	12.60.	[0.80]
No. 213.	" " 9 " "	18.20.	[1.20]
No. 214.	" " 12 " "	23.50.	[1.60]
No. 214b.	" " 20 " "	52.00.	[4.00]

The Lettering on the foregoing Plain Globes is in English, except on the 20" Globe on which it is in German.

IMPORTED GLOBES, MAPS, etc.

Indestructible Plain Globes.
b.) Celestial.

These Celestial Globes represent the stars of the first seven magnitudes according to their present positions. The heavens are of a light blue tint, the twelve signs of the zodiac appear relief-like. (The names are in German.)

I. *On stand of black polished wood.*

No. 192a.	Celestial Globe,	7″ Diameter	3.30.	[0.65]
No. 193a.	"	" 9″ "	5.50.	[0.80]
No. 194a.	"	" 12″ "	7.50.	[1.20]

II. *With graduated brass half-meridian.*

No. 197a.	Celestial Globe,	7″ Diameter	5.30.	[0.65]
No. 198a.	"	" 9″ "	8.20.	[0.80]
No. 199a.	"	" 12″ "	11.50.	[1.20]

III. *With horizon, graduated full meridian, hour-circle, quadrant and compass.*

No. 212a.	Celestial Globe.	7″ Diameter	12.60.	[0.80]
No. 213a.	"	" 9″ "	18.20.	[1.20]
No. 214a.	"	" 12″ "	23.50.	[1.60]

Tellurians with Lunaria.

Plastic representations of the movements of the Earth and Moon round the Sun.

a) Tellurian with rotary gear.

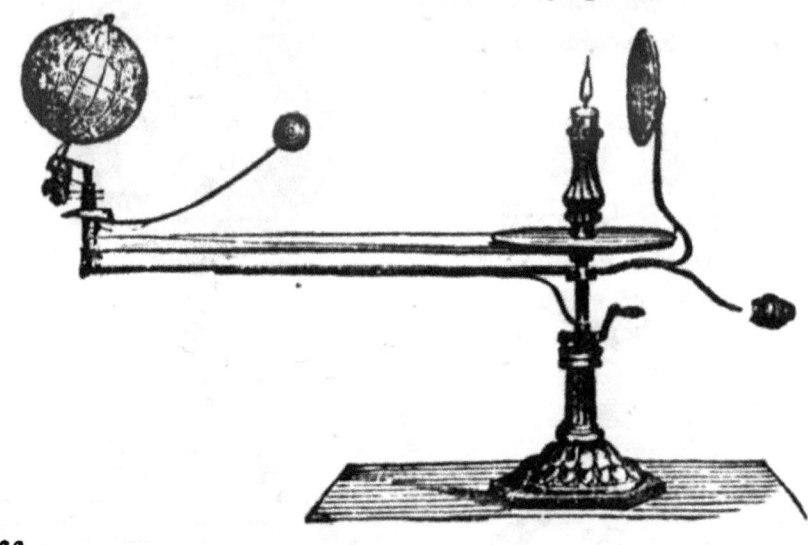

No. 266 a. Tellurian No. 0 with 1″ Globe, 12″ Diam. of Earth's orbit.	5.25.	[0.50]
No. 266. " " 1 " 2″ " 18″ " " "	12.00.	[0.75]
No. 267. " " 2 " 3″ " 30″ " " "	18.00.	[1.25]
No. 268. " " 3 " 5″ " 40″ " " "	24.00.	[2.00]
No. 269. " " 4 " 7″ " 54″ " " "	50.00.	[4.00]

b) Tellurians with clockwork.

No. 271. Tellurian No. 5 with Terrestrial Globe 5″	68.00.	[3.00]
No. 271a. " " 6 " " " 3″	44.00.	[1.75]

Planetarium.

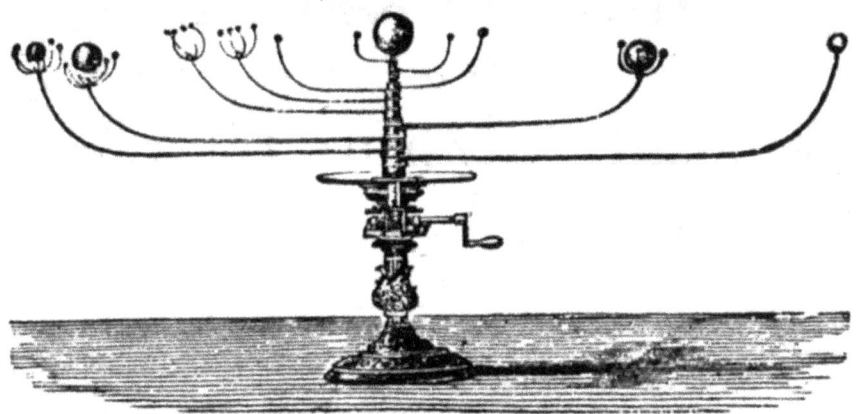

No. 272. **Planetarium** on elegant pedestal frame, showing the movements of the Planets with their satellites round the Sun. The Planets are distinguished by differences of size and color; and their motions relative to each other are indicated. This apparatus is set in operation by clockwork.   130.00. [1.50]

No. 273.   The same, without clockwork (with rotary gear).   44.00. [1.25]

Dr. Hermann Berghaus'
Chart of the World

containing the lines of Oceanic Mail Steam Communication and Overland Routes, the International Aerial and Sub-marine Telegraphs, and the principal tracks of Sailing Vessels; presenting some Continental surface characteristics, the Oceanic currents and important Deep-sea Soundings. With 25 additional Charts and Plans showing the general Currents of air, and the lines of equal magnetic variation, the Tehuantepec, Honduras, Nicaragua, Panama, Darien, and Suez Routes, several Seaports, the Telegraphic and Steam lines round the World.

In 8 sheets, together measuring 61 by 38 inches.

Price $5.00.

Mounted on muslin for a Wall-Map, varnished, with rollers.

Price $11.00 (Packing in Box 75 cents extra).

    The estimation in which this Chart is held is best shown not only by its having attained, in 1871, its sixth edition, but by the fact that the United States Government purchase large quantities for the use of Departments.

    Important improvements and the latest details of information have considerably enhanced the value of the *Chart of the World*. It is equally well adapted to the *Counting-house*, the *School-room* and the *Library*. Intrinsic worth, external beauty, and moderation of price commend it to the public.

E. Steiger's
Systematic Catalogues
OF
Standard German Literature.

Any of these Catalogues sent *free* to persons desirous of receiving them.

Steiger's Fest-Catalog. Verzeichniss einer Auswahl *gebundener deutscher Bücher*, welche sich besonders zu *Festgeschenken* eignen.—(**Festival Catalogue.** A Selection of *Bound German Books* suitable for *Presents*.)

61 pp. Contents: a) **Complete and Collected Works** (Editions of German Classics, &c.) b) **Romances, Novels, Tales.** c) **Poems.** d) **Anthologies in Poetry and Prose.** (Selected Thoughts, Sayings, Poems, &c.) e) **Dramatic Works.** f) **Illustrated Editions.**—Kaulbach's Illustrations to Goethe and Schiller. Splendidly illustrated Poems or Illustrations without the Text. Editions with Chromolithographic Illustrations. Miscellaneous Works Illustrated. Splendid Editions of the Bible and Illustrated Religious Works. g) **Histories.** Biographies. Correspondence. Memoirs. Archæological and Mythological Works. h) **Works on Literature, Art, Æsthetics, Music.** i) **Geographical and Ethnographical Works.** Voyages and Travels. Atlases. Maps. k) **Works on Natural Sciences.** (Chemistry, Pharmacy, Botany, Horticulture.) l) **Works on Commerce.** m) **Encyclopædias. Dictionaries.** 1. Encyclopædias. 2. Dictionaries of the German Language. 3. Dictionaries of Foreign Words and Synonyms. 4. Dictionaries of German and one other Language. 5. English Dictionaries with one other Language. 6. Dictionaries in Various Languages. Polyglot Dictionaries. n) **Works on Female Education.—Cookery.—Housewifery.—Domestic Management.**—*Abbreviations explained.*

Steiger's Theologische Bibliothek. I. Systematische Zusammenstellung deutscher Schriften aus dem Gebiete der *Protestantischen Theologie.* — (**Theological Library.** No. I. A Systematic Catalogue of German Publications in the Department of *Protestant Theology.*)

68 pp. Contents: I. **Bibliography. Collected Works.** II. **Works Introductory to Theology.** III. **The Bible.** a) Editions of the Bible and its Parts. b) Biblical Exegetics. c) Sciences bearing on Biblical Exegesis. (1. Biblical Encyclopædias.—Concordances.—Biblical Linguistics. 2. Biblical Introductory Studies. 3. Lives of Jesus and the Apostles. 4. Biblical History and Archæology. 5. Biblical Geography.—Travels in Palestine. d) Biblical Theology.) IV. **Historical Theology.** a) History of Churches and Dogmas. b) Biographies. Memoirs. Correspondence. c) Sects. d) Patristic Theology. e) Apologetics. Polemics. Symbolics. V. **Systematic Theology.** VI. **Practical Theology.** a) General Expositions. Homiletics. b) Worship and Hymnology. c) Catechetics and Religious Instruction. d) Home and Foreign Missions. e) Church Policy and Laws.

f) Religious Contentions and Controversies. VII. Sermons and Religious Discourses. VIII. Popular Devotional Works. a) in Prose. b) in Verse.—*Abbreviations explained. List of Authors.*

Steiger's Philosophische Bibliothek.
Systematische Zusammenstellung deutscher Schriften aus dem Gebiete der *Philosophie* und *Æsthetik*. — (**Philosophical Library.** A Systematic Catalogue of German Publications in the Departments of *Philosophy* and *Æsthetics*.)

39 pp. Contents. **I. General Division.** A) *Historico-Literary Works.* a) General Histories of Philosophy. b), c) Histories of Philosophy before the Christian Era.—Greek Philosophy. d) Histories of Philosophy of the Christian Era. (1., 2. Patristic and Scholastic Philosophy.—Hebrew—Arabic Philosophy. 3. Modern Philosophy.) B) *Discursive Works.* a) Systematic. (Formal and Scientific Encyclopædias, Special Introductory Works and other Treatises on Philosophy in general.) b) Miscellaneous Writings. (Complete Works, Collected Works, Commentaries.) **II. Particular Division.** A) *Theoretical or Speculative Philosophy.* a) Elementary Books. b) Logic. c) Metaphysics. Natural Philosophy. (Inclusive of Works on Materialism.) e) Psychology and Anthropology. (1. Philosophical Systems, Manuals, and General Treatises. 2. Special Writings, Mental Faculties. [Mnemonics.] 3. Anthropognosis. [Phrenology.] Pneumatology. [Spiritism.] B) *Practical Philosophy.* a) Introductory Works generally. Elementary Books. Systematized Writings. b) Natural Law. c) Ethics or Moral Philosophy. d) Art of Life. e) Philosophy of Religion. C) *Æsthetics.*—*Abbreviations explained.—List of Authors.*

Steiger's Pädagogische Bibliothek.
Systematische Zusammenstellung deutscher Schriften über die *Theorie der Erziehung* und *des Unterrichts*.—(**Pedagogical Library.** A Systematic Catalogue of German Publications on the *Theory of Education* and *Instruction*.)

41 pp. Contents: **I. Bibliography and Encyclopædia of Pedagogy.** Collected Works. Anthologies. **II. General Pedagogy**; Systems (Handbooks of Pedagogy); Home Instruction; Discipline; Miscellaneous Writings on General Pedagogy. **III. Pedagogy Proper.** Anthropology; Psychology; Logic (Æsthetics); Physical Development—School-Dietetics; Female Education—Female Handicraft; Education of Orphans—of Neglected Children—of Weak-minded Children; Education of the Blind -of the Deaf and Dumb; the Kindergarten and Infant-Teaching; Elementary and Object Lessons; Public Schools; Supplementary and High School—Colleges; Seminaries—Education of Teachers—General Method of Instruction; Universities—School Management. **IV. School Systems in different States. V. History of Pedagogy and School Systems**; Biographies and Memoirs. *Abbreviations explained.*

Steiger's Catalog deutscher Bilderbücher und Jugendschriften.
Nach Altersstufen geordnet.—(**Catalogue of German Picture Books and Juveniles** classified according to the age of children.

49 pp. Contents: **I. Juveniles for children from 3 to 8 years of age.** a) Picture Books without Text. b) ABC, Spelling and Reading Books. c) Fables, Poems, and Stories. **II. Juveniles for children from 8 to 11 years of age. III. Juveniles for children from 11 to 15 years of age. IV. Books for young ladies. V. Games.** ☞ A large number of these books are well adapted to Sunday School Libraries, &c.

Steiger's Medicinische Bibliothek. Systematische Zusammenstellung deutscher Schriften aus dem Gesammtgebiete der *Medicin, Pharmacie, Pharmacologie* und *Pharmacognosie.* (**Medical Library.** A Systematic Catalogue of German Publications in the Departments of *Medicine, Pharmacy, Pharmacology* and *Pharmacognosy.*)

<small>82 pp. Contents. I. **Anatomy and Physiology.** (4 Subdivisions.) II. **General Medicine.** (6 Subdivisions.) III. **Materia Medica. Forensic Medicine, Climato- and Balneo-Therapeutics. Veterinary Medicine,** etc. (7 Subdivisions.) IV. **Internal Medicine.** (11 Subdivisions.) V. **External Medicine.** (8 Subdivisions.) VI. **Gynecology and Pædiatrics.** (3 Subdivisions.) VII. **Homeopathy.** VIII. **Medical and Pharmaceutical Periodicals.** (2 Subdivisions.)—*Index of Authors.*</small>

Steiger's Zeitschriften-Liste. Eine systematisch geordnete Zusammenstellung der *periodischen Erscheinungen der deutschen Literatur* im Jahre 1872. (List of *Standard Periodicals of German Literature* in the year 1872.)

<small>30 pp. Contents. I. Bibliography. Literary and Critical Periodicals. II a. Protestant Theology. II b. Catholic Theology. II c. Jewish Literature and Theology. II d. German-Catholic, Liberal, and Mennonite Theology. II e. Freemasonry. III. Philosophy. IV a. Education. IV b. Periodicals for Youth. IV c. Gymnastics. V. Languages, Philology. VI. History. Geography. Statistics. Numismatics. Archaeology. VII. Politics. Contemporary Events. Social Questions. VIII. Jurisprudence. Polity, Cameralistics. IX. Mathematics. Astronomy. X. Military Science. Hippology. XI. Architecture. Engineering. Nautical Science. XII. Forestry and Huntsmanship. XIII. Domestic and Rural Economy. Horticulture. XIV. Commerce. XV. Technology. Mechanics. Manufactures. XVI. Mining and Metallurgy. XVII. Natural Sciences. XVIII. Natural Philosophy. Chemistry. Pharmacy. XIX. Medicine. Surgery. Obstetrics, Midwifery. XX. Veterinary Art. XXI. Fashions, Fancy and Plain Needle-work. Female Education. XXII. Belles Lettres, Entertaining Literature. XXIII. Music. Art. Theatre. Chess. XXIV. Stenography, Phonography. XXV. Miscellaneous.
Political and Local Papers published in all parts of Germany, Switzerland, etc.</small>

Steiger's New Illustrated Descriptive School Book Catalogue.

German Dialects. A List of 400 Publications representing a majority of the *Dialects* spoken in the German Empire.

Philology, chiefly comparative. A Catalogue of valuable Books on *Comparative Philology,* in English, German, and French.

Numerous other Catalogues are in preparation.

A rich store of Bibliographical Material enables me promptly to furnish information concerning literary works published in all parts of the World.

E. Steiger.